Creative Block Play

Creative Block Play

A Comprehensive Guide to Learning through Building

Rosanne Regan Hansel
Foreword by Margie Carter

Redleaf Press®
www.redleafpress.org
800-423-8309

Published by Redleaf Press
10 Yorkton Court
St. Paul, MN 55117

First edition 2017
Cover design by Erin Kirk New
Cover photograph by Gillham Studios
Interior design by Percolator
Typeset in Sentinel
Printed in the United States of America
23 22 21 20 19 18 17 16   1 2 3 4 5 6 7 8

Library of Congress Cataloging-in-Publication Data

Names: Hansel, Rosanne Regan, author.
Title: Creative block play / Rosanne Regan Hansel.
Description: First edition. | St. Paul, MN : Redleaf Press, [2016] | Includes
    bibliographical references and index.
Identifiers: LCCN 2016013821 (print) | LCCN 2016026309 (ebook) | ISBN
    9781605544458 (pbk. : acid-free paper) | ISBN 9781605544465 (ebook)
Subjects: LCSH: Block building (Children's activity) | Early childhood
    education.
Classification: LCC LB1139.C7 H36 2016 (print) | LCC LB1139.C7 (ebook) | DDC
    371.33/7--dc23
LC record available at https://lccn.loc.gov/2016013821

Printed on acid-free paper

To my family—Dave, Amber, Andy, Jenn, Emily, Jeff, and Dagan—
for teaching me so much about what it means to love, laugh,
accept, create, and build.

Contents

1

Understanding the Benefits of Block Play

2

Preparing the Environment for Block Play

3

Exploring Possibilities through Block Play

4

Supporting Children during Block Play

5

Guiding Deeper Engagement in Block Play

Acknowledgments

My life's work has been shaped by memorable encounters with a number of remarkable people, many of whom you will become more familiar with in these pages. First and foremost, I thank the administrators, teachers, and children from the public schools of New Jersey who made this book possible. I have been genuinely inspired by kindergarten and preschool teachers Kathleen Spadola and Nicole Dennis from Paterson, New Jersey; kindergarten teacher Krista Crumrine from Union City School District; preschool teacher Marianne Cane from Englewood School District; master teachers Virginia Sacchi and Mary Ann Sanguinito from Phillipsburg School District; master teacher Sally Kacar and preschool teacher Arlene Calafut (now retired) from New Brunswick School District; and Principal Bonita Samuels and her teachers from the School District of South Orange–Maplewood. They have demonstrated that creative block play is entirely compatible with a standards-based curriculum and performance-based assessment. In addition to public preschools in New Jersey, the college children's centers at Kean University and William Paterson University offer early childhood students the opportunity to gain experience in high-quality classrooms. My deepest thanks to Sonja de Groot Kim and Cindy Gennarelli for their careful documentation of block play in those centers.

The Quakers (or Friends) began educating women and people of color in the United States long before education was considered a right. The work of Quaker educators helped me understand that the role of education is to help all children find their unique voice and to use that voice, or special ability, to contribute something of value to the world in order to make it a better place for all to live. As a preschool director at Abington Friends School, I had the privilege of hiring an outstanding young lady, Tamara Clark (now at the Parent Infant Center in Philadelphia), and years later, of hearing her present with her colleagues at a NAEYC conference on the topic of their newly built outdoor classroom. Tamara generously contributed photos of children's indoor and outdoor explorations with blocks and other construction materials to this book. These photos and inspiration from Rusty Keeler's book *Natural Playscapes* highlight the importance of outdoor learning, which I believe children need more than ever today.

Visiting the world-renowned schools of Reggio Emilia, Italy, and meeting Loris Malaguzzi, Carlina Rinaldi, Lella Gandini, Amelia Gambetti, and the Reggio teachers was a life-changing experience for me. Thank you Tracy Keyes and Judy Leigh, for being eager travelers with me on this inspirational journey. I have devoured every article, book, video, and exhibit about this creative educational approach and have traveled far and wide to see Reggio-inspired schools in the United States. After spending an enlightening day at the Boulder Journey School in Boulder, Colorado, several years ago, I invited Alison Maher and her teachers to contribute documentation on block play for this book, and I was delighted that they accepted. More recently, during a tour of the Universal Studios Child Care Center managed by Bright Horizons in Los Angeles, California, with Program Coordinator Janette Deddio, I was struck by their breathtakingly beautiful outdoor classrooms and building materials. Many thanks to Janette and Program Director Jennifer West for allowing me to include photos from their extraordinary center in this book.

Margie Carter and Deb Curtis may never know the influence they have had on me as an administrator of early childhood programs, a provider of professional development, an adviser on early childhood environments, and a shaper of early childhood policy. Their workshops, videos, and books have had a powerful impact on my work, which you will see throughout this book. Margie led a study tour of early childhood programs in Auckland, New Zealand, where I was reminded that it is entirely possible to put children, families, and joyful learning at the center of early childhood education and at the same time offer the highest-quality learning experiences for young children. Margie Carter and Deb Curtis's *Designs for Living and Learning* has become an invaluable resource in my presentations on classroom environments.

When I was the lone art educator working in an elementary school many years ago, the National Art Education Association conferences kept me inspired. It was at one of these conferences that I first attended a workshop by Cathy Weisman Topal and discovered her books. Cathy's *Beautiful Stuff! Learning with Found Materials* remains a favorite in my workshops with kindergarten teachers and was the inspiration for Katie Spadola's exploration with found materials in this book. Katie has been instrumental in providing insight and feedback on the content of this book so that it will be a practical and useful guide for teachers. Working with Katie these past few years has given me renewed hope in the next generation of educators and leaders in the early childhood field. I am so grateful to Katie for her energy and determination to be a positive role model for teachers through the examples she shares in this book and in her presentations.

My entrance to the world of science and math occurred when I was hired as the early childhood specialist for the Math Science Partnership (MSP) at Rutgers University, funded by the National Science Foundation. I am forever grateful for having had the opportunity to train with the authors of the Young Scientist Series on *Building Structures with Young Children*, Jeffrey Winokur, Karen Worth, and Ingrid Chalufour, and to learn from the MSP science specialist, Hector Lopez, and Jorie Quinn, director of the early childhood programs at the Liberty Science Center at that time. This experience expanded my understanding of the extraordinary connections among science, technology, engineering, art, and mathematics—a network of connections that now has a name: STEAM.

Working in the arena of government educational policy is both unbelievably challenging and richly rewarding. My colleagues over the years, especially Elizabeth Vaughan and Pam Brillante, have been tireless collaborators in ensuring that every child in New Jersey has the best possible start in life with a high-quality preschool education. I give a special nod of appreciation to my colleague James DeSimone for his expertise and feedback on the ECERS-3 guidelines on the block area included in chapter 2. I am proud to be working in a state that promotes developmentally appropriate practices when so many preschool and kindergarten classrooms are under tremendous pressure to look more and more like first and second grades. It has been important to all of us that materials like blocks remain in the early childhood classroom.

I owe an endless debt of gratitude to my friend and fellow author Karen Nemeth, who not only introduced me to my agent but also encouraged me through every phase of this book. In the days before my first draft was due, I asked Karen why she ever decided to write another book, knowing how impossibly time consuming it was to write the first. "Rosanne," she laughed, "it's like having a baby. After you go through labor, you think you will never do it again. But then you forget the pain and go ahead and do it again anyway!"

A very special thanks to my agent, MaryAnn Kohl, whose wonderful sense of humor, understanding, and guidance made the early stages of this endeavor feel less painful than I expected. My deepest appreciation goes to my editors at Redleaf Press, Kyra Ostendorf, Kara Lomen, Christine Zuchora-Walske, and Douglas Schmitz for their patience and support in helping a novice navigate through the book writing and editing process. You all taught me so much!

Thank you to my niece, Christy Breiby, for her photo contribution to this book, to my neighbors Ian and Xander for allowing me to observe and photograph their block play, and to my mother and siblings—Mildred, Mark, Mary, Janis, Dick, Peggy,

Carol, Dan, and John—for providing me with incredible opportunities to play and learn in my early years. I give a great big heartfelt thank-you and hug to my husband, Dave, for making sure I never went hungry and for providing me with quiet time to write, and to my daughters, Amber and Emily, for their kindest words of encouragement from beginning to end. Finally, the recent birth of my first grandson, Dagan, inspired and motivated me to complete this book so that he, and every child, can experience the pleasure and benefits of creative block play.

Foreword

by Margie Carter

Take a minute to do some unconventional thinking. Imagine you could only set up one area in your classroom. What would that be? Can you imagine a space that would allow for a variety of learning experiences to come together, including children's sensory integration needs and the active body movement that builds critical brain connections? In your hands is a book to stir your imagination. Rosanne Hansel offers a strong case for creating a building area as the central feature of any early childhood classroom. This idea is especially compelling because children today have little time for outdoor active exploration. While we work to change that reality, it is critical to offer an expansive indoor space for block play to support learning and brain development, as well as create joyful childhood experiences.

If you follow the research on play, the interconnectedness of all learning domains, and the growing recognition of the skills required for the twenty-first century, the benefits of block play are undisputable. Why then, in the name of school readiness, is block play marginalized, if not disappearing from children's classrooms? When adequate time and space for block play *are* provided, why is it primarily for children in more privileged settings? Do we think children in publicly funded programs are less deserving or less capable of learning through all the opportunities that playing with blocks offer? Evidence is mounting that we have an opportunity gap that is increasing, rather than closing the achievement gap (Gramling 2015). The right to play has become an equity issue (Jordan 2016).

To be sure, early childhood standards and best practices say that play is how children learn best, and Environmental Rating Scales (ERS) describe how block areas should be set up in classrooms. But does that mean teachers and parents see the connections between brain development, school readiness, and adequate time, space, and materials for play in the block area? Do they truly understand how a well-provisioned building area reinforces learning across domains, helps with visual spatial learning, and supports the all-important sensory-active-body-brain-growing work of young children? If not, put a copy of this book in their hands. Encourage and trust teachers to begin researching and documenting what unfolds. Give them time to study their documentation and connect what they see children doing with blocks to learning domains and desired outcomes.

Notice how they are more intellectually and emotionally engaged in their work. You'll find examples of what Lilian Katz refers to as teachers meeting up with children's minds. Occupying the block area enhances their excitement about learning along with the children.

Perhaps we don't see adequate space and time given to block play because teachers are given confusing messages about school readiness and basically aren't trusted to adequately provide for children's learning. Instead, with no extra time or pay, they are given a boatload of required, discrete lessons to deliver—everything from nutrition to gun safety to empathy, math, science, literacy, and language development. All of their teaching has to be documented with data on the children's progress. Publicly funded programs and state Quality Rating and Improvement System (QRIS) organizations say play is important, yet they typically require the adoption of an approved commercial "research based" curriculum and assessment tools. Teachers get the message that these curricular mandates are the priority—attached to measurable outcomes that generate needed dollars. They don't understand that too much seat work is literally hazardous to brain development (Hanscom 2016; Ayres 2005). With too much to fit into their daily schedule, teachers trim away extended time for open-ended exploration of blocks. It's unlikely that children will invest or get to deeper learning with only fifteen minutes of free time, limits on how many can play in the block area, and constant reminders to be careful and clean up.

It's true that some children thrive in free play environments, while others don't initially do well. Effective educators know that not all children can easily just play, especially in today's screen-filled world. Approaches to learning and cognitive styles vary individually and culturally. A child growing up in a cultural context that teaches you to wait to be told what to do or to watch for cues the adult gives for behavior might be unsure how to engage in play where self-initiation is valued or expected. Children deserve a culturally competent teacher to partner with their family. When children come to our programs with limited self-initiated play skills, teachers must diligently find their home or community-based funds of knowledge to tap into as a scaffold for expanding play skills. They must recognize different cognitive and cultural learning styles and position themselves to support how each child learns best.

Inequities stemming from racism and differences in economic and educational opportunities mean that some families don't believe playing will give their children the leg up they need to be successful. Neither these families nor play should be dismissed. Racism and poverty are endemic and systemic, and these families need us as their allies. We have to understand the opportunity gaps before we can effectively overcome the achievement gap. And among the many opportunities for an equity agenda is children's right to play. Kristie Norwood reminds us: "Poverty creates restrictions for people. Why would you put a child in a more constricted situation by eliminating time to learn from play? Why would you not feed their brains with opportunities to explore and investigate? While the condition of poverty must be addressed, children deserve the benefit of quality, enriched experiences. All children deserve engaged learning experiences and children affected by poverty, more so" (Carter and Norwood 2016, 12).

The deeper, complex play from which children benefit has to be understood and intentionally planned by teachers. Therein lies the value of this comprehensive guide Rosanne Hansel has assembled. As you read, you'll learn more about how to prepare the environment for children's engagement and expand your thinking about ways to meet standards and exceed desired outcomes. You'll discover not only that children will be learning as they build, converse, work with schema, negotiate, and problem solve; you, too, will be learning—discovering what you are curious about, how you can better understand children's efforts, and how to focus less on their behaviors and more on their ideas. The principles, visual examples, and illuminating stories here will prompt you to more thoughtfully consider your role in supporting children's deeper learning. You may find yourself spotting some non-traditional materials that could bring new possibilities to your building area. The idea of observing and documenting might shift from being a chore to an excitement for you with so many stories unfolding in block play. Your interactions with children will likely shift from language development techniques to more genuine conversations where you are naming your curiosities and describing what you see being tried and achieved. Expanded outcomes for children will likely include more delight and satisfaction with their accomplishments; and incidentally, more meaningful and sophisticated vocabulary, along with stronger connections between diverse interests, ideas, and people. Exemplary stories of children and teachers in *Creative Block Play* serve as a testimony to this.

One of my favorite children's books about building is Christy Hale's *Dreaming Up: A Celebration of Building* (2012), where illustrations of children's building structures are matched with photographs of innovative architecture around the world. The book's theme and creative spirit, "If they can dream it, they can build it," is my wish for teachers. Dream big. Be bold. Build innovation into your teaching.

Moving block play to the center of your thinking about curriculum holds great promise for learning together with young children. This incredibly valuable book will help you rethink and reimagine possibilities. Consider it a call to action.

Introduction

> All people—and I mean scholars, researchers, and teachers, who in any place have set themselves to study children seriously—have ended up discovering not so much the limits and weaknesses of children but rather their surprising and extraordinary strengths and capabilities linked with an inexhaustible need for expression and realization.
>
> **Loris Malaguzzi,** *The Hundred Languages of Children*

I grew up in a large family in South Carolina during a time when outdoor play was what all kids did after school and during the summer. When I think back, I don't remember the intense summer heat, stopping to eat, or missing favorite TV shows. What I do remember is climbing trees, building forts, playing dodgeball and softball in the street, putting on shows, designing clothing and houses for my dolls, riding my bicycle, and playing for hours on a patch of dirt, building cities and roadways with whatever materials we could find—old bricks, sticks, scraps of wood, rusty roller skates, stones, a few wheeled toys, but mainly relying on our imaginations.

Although I enjoyed the solitude that nature offered away from my noisy family, most of these activities occurred with my siblings and neighbors. So like it or not, I developed the ability to negotiate, take turns, play fair, muster some grit, lose gracefully, and get along with a wide range of personalities. Even though I did not attend preschool or kindergarten, I entered school more than ready to settle down to the academic challenges of first grade.

Most children today do not have the same play opportunities I had. It may be because it's not safe outdoors or because there is too much competition from screen time and organized activities. Whatever the reason, the result is that in my workshops with teachers, I am hearing more and more stories about how young children are having a tough time socially in group situations and often don't know how to play with others. These stories are verified in the growing body of research from psychologists, pediatricians, and organizations like the Alliance for Childhood, Defending the Early Years, and the National Association for the Education of Young Children (NAEYC).

My own concern, as a former art educator, is that without physical play (large-muscle and fine-motor skills), hand-eye coordination and visual-spatial skills are diminishing in children. In short, young children are having fewer three-dimensional, hands-on experiences at home and, sadly, very little in school and some child care settings. As I visit kindergarten classrooms around the state, I am seeing too much time spent in front of two-dimensional screens and workbooks or worksheets that offer children few sensory experiences or opportunities for deep thinking and creative problem solving.

The present-day laser-like focus on language, literacy, and math skills learned primarily through paper-and-pencil tasks that typically have one right answer contradicts what we know about how young children learn. Current research has greatly expanded our understanding of healthy child development and brain development (Copple and Bredekamp 2009; Wellhousen and Kieff 2001). Children's learning is strongly influenced by stimulating and enriching environments that offer them the opportunity to manipulate three-dimensional materials; practice oral language skills; hear and use new vocabulary; translate abstract ideas into concrete constructions; persist at solving problems; develop visual-spatial skills, imagination, and creativity; and engage and collaborate with peers. This is best done in a play-based environment stocked with a variety of blocks, accessories, and other interesting materials.

As education writer Susan Engel (2015) recently said, we seem not to be able to put this research into practice when "everyone is worried about whether kids are 'learning what they need' [for getting] into college, finding good jobs, getting along in a big company, and learning new trades. The country's whole school system seems geared toward solving large-scale economic woes and producing future workers. It's most definitely not geared toward children."

With the national focus on twenty-first-century skills such as creativity, problem solving, and collaboration (see pages 13–14), you would think that the early childhood focus on creative, play-based classrooms would be in the spotlight. Instead, what we are seeing is a growing trend of preschool and kindergarten classrooms that look more like the upper grades. Administrators scramble to ensure that young children are meeting all the standards using a one-size-fits-all curriculum and inappropriate assessments, therefore putting unnecessary pressures on teachers and young children. The pressures on the hurried child that developmental psychologist David Elkind wrote about more than thirty years ago have increased today. Much has changed since then, but what has not changed, according to Elkind

(2009), is the age at which young children learn to walk, talk, and read, despite our efforts to introduce these skills earlier.

Like Elkind, many early childhood teachers, educators, and psychologists are concerned that young children are not having free and spontaneous play experiences at home and so are entering early childhood settings with poorly developed play skills (Almon 2013; Nell, Drew, and Bush 2013). What that means for those who care for and teach young children is that it becomes even more critical to provide a wide range of open-ended learning materials, such as blocks, that provide creative possibilities to challenge, stimulate, and engage children's thinking rather than providing meaningless tasks that don't always accomplish that goal (Grossman 1996). It may also mean that teachers will need to offer more time and supports for children as they learn to make smart choices about where they want to play and whom they want to play with, and plan for what they want to do once their choices are made.

In my most recent work at the New Jersey Department of Education, gathering research on twenty-first-century skills, brain development, and how children approach learning, it has become increasingly apparent to me that social, emotional, and cognitive development are not discrete domains but are absolutely interconnected. We now know that other skills and approaches to learning, such as taking initiative, engaging in and persisting at a task, collaborating and communicating successfully with others, exercising the imagination, identifying and solving problems, making connections between ideas, concepts, and subjects, and applying newly learned information to new situations, are critical skills for young children (and adults) in today's world. When learning addresses the whole child, it both prepares the child for the future and embraces the needs of the child.

Creative block play may seem an unlikely way to reverse the current trends in early childhood education that ignore the research on how young children learn. However, as a Bank Street College of Education graduate steeped in the importance of unit blocks introduced by Caroline Pratt many years ago, as an educator who has seen and been transformed by the preschools of Reggio Emilia and their counterparts in New Zealand and America, and as an early childhood specialist who has worked with science and math specialists and who has provided teachers with professional development on the importance of block building, I am convinced that block play is essential for every child's creative, social-emotional, cognitive, and physical development.

Whether you are a teacher educator, a teacher, a child care provider, a parent of young children, or one of the growing number of adults homeschooling your children, you will find creative and practical ideas and resources in this book to guide you in making the most of children's experiences with blocks. I hope you will be convinced, as I am, that blocks offer young children enormous benefits. In the following chapters, you will hear stories from teachers working with three-, four-, and five-year-olds in a variety of settings—public preschools and kindergartens, college lab schools, and private child care centers and schools—who have contributed remarkable visual documentation of children's play with blocks, including their practical strategies for setting up the environment, providing children with encouragement and support in several domains (physical, cognitive, and social-emotional), offering interesting new materials to enhance creativity in their block play, and intentionally planning for and providing ample time to deepen children's investigations with blocks.

These teachers truly demonstrate the art of teaching as they find the balance between rigorous and playful learning, revealing children's "surprising and extraordinary strengths and capabilities" (Malaguzzi 1993a, 72). I hope you will be inspired by the photos and stories you find here and that you will return to this book again and again to see the endless possibilities of learning through and playing with blocks.

Understanding the Benefits of Block Play

> The pleasure of blocks stems primarily from the aesthetic experience. It involves the whole person—muscles and senses, intellect and emotion, individual growth and social interaction. Learning results from the imaginative activity, from the need to pose and solve problems.
>
> **Elisabeth S. Hirsch,** *The Block Book*

THE VALUE OF BUILDING WITH BLOCKS

Blocks are one of the greatest investments you can make for your child, classroom, or program. Why? Simply put, they will provide a lifetime of benefits rarely attributed to any other material or toy designed for young children. Early childhood experts who have studied young children's play with blocks, such as Harriet Johnson, Elisabeth Hirsch, Mary Jo Pollman, and Karyn Tunks, have written extensively about the range of skills that young children develop from block play. They each offer evidence that when children are given time to plan, construct, and create with blocks, they develop socially, emotionally, cognitively, and physically (Hirsch 1996; Pollman 2010; Tunks 2009, 2013; Wellhousen and Kieff 2001).

What can young children do with blocks?
- carry blocks
- fill and empty containers of blocks
- make enclosures
- stack or make towers
- build bridges
- create patterns and symmetry
- make representations
- name structures
- reproduce real-life structures
- engage in pretend play
- change the shape and arrangement of objects
- describe positions, directions, and distances when building
- observe people, places, and things from different spatial viewpoints
- fit things together and take them apart
- interpret spatial relations in drawings, pictures, and photographs

Learning through Play

> The importance of play has been recognized in all cultures; it has been widely studied and endorsed in the human sciences and demonstrated in practice in enlightened schools throughout the world. And yet, the standards movement in many countries treats play as a trivial and expendable extra in schools—a distraction from the serious business of studying and passing tests. The exile of play is one of the great tragedies of standardized education.
>
> **Ken Robinson and Lou Aronica, *Creative Schools***

Many early childhood educators and parents associate play with fun classroom experiences such as listening to stories, coloring or painting, having snack, playing dress-up, and playing with toys, with no expectation that young children could be more challenged intellectually. At the other end of the spectrum, there are early childhood classrooms that emphasize more formal instruction with a focus on academic skills, such as learning the alphabet, days of the week, names of the month, and counting. Many of those academic skills are focused on literacy and numeracy skills, disconnected from young children's life experiences. Those skills are typically practiced in worksheets and other paper-and-pencil activities relying mostly on memorization or copying with one correct answer. But early childhood experts, such as Lilian Katz, argue that learning can be both fun and challenging without resorting to inappropriate paper-and-pencil activities. Katz says that in the early years, children must be offered "a wide range of experiences, opportunities, resources and contexts that will provoke, stimulate, and support children's innate intellectual dispositions" (2015, 1). She believes that one of the best ways to provide this is through projects or long-term investigations, which are featured in chapter 5.

According to Lev Vygotsky, "Play is the most important factor in children's development . . . play becomes the means for developing self-regulation; the child learns to set aside personal needs in order to find satisfaction through the continuation of play. . . . Because imaginary play involves symbolism, such play facilitates the development of symbolic and abstract thought" (Nell, Drew, and Bush 2013, 13).

Like scientists, young children are curious and are continually exploring their worlds in order to make sense of the unknown. Through playful experiments, they learn from both their mistakes and their successes. Like artists, they find ways to express their ideas through imaginative play, trying out new roles, media, and materials. It is often said that children's play is their work, and while they take it

very seriously, they also find it immensely enjoyable. If we want young children to take risks and learn from their mistakes, then we have to be sure to provide plenty of opportunities throughout the day for using open-ended materials like blocks that offer more than one right way to use them in a playful, experimental way.

Developing Social-Emotional Skills

When teachers are asked what social-emotional skills they want young children to have in order to be successful in school and in life, they quickly generate a list that includes the top five many agree they want children to know:

1. How to recognize and express feelings
2. How to self-regulate: focus attention and control impulses
3. How to listen and empathize
4. How to make friends, enter into play, and share
5. How to solve problems

Basing their observations on the work of Vygotsky, researchers Elena Bodrova and Deborah Leong say that early childhood educators can help young children develop strong social-emotional skills by supporting high-quality pretend play

as a key medium for learning. Vygotsky illustrated that when children spend time playing make-believe, they develop a critical cognitive skill called executive function. One aspect of executive function is self-regulation—the ability to purposefully monitor your own behaviors (Bodrova and Leong 2005).

During creative block play, children learn to practice self-regulation as well as the other social skills teachers most want to see children learn. There are specific examples throughout this book of young children learning how to enter play, share with others, listen respectfully, understand different perspectives as they try out new roles, focus their attention for extended periods of time, express their ideas and feelings appropriately, and independently or collaboratively solve complex problems. In my experience, this play-based learning works far better than providing rewards or

incentives to achieve the social-emotional development goals that occur naturally through play. Children who are actively engaged in these interesting, hands-on experiences rarely exhibit challenging behaviors.

Reinforcing Language and Literacy

> Adults tend to talk about learning as if it were medicine: unpleasant, but necessary and good for you. Why not instead think of learning as if it were food—something so valuable to humans that they have evolved to experience it as a pleasure? The more a person likes fresh, healthy food, the more likely that individual is to have a good diet. Why can't it be the same with learning? Let children learn because they love to.
> **Susan Engel, "Joy: A Subject Schools Lack"**

Learning to speak, read, and write doesn't have to be a painful process. When young children are deeply engaged in creative block play, they are highly motivated to communicate with teachers and with each other about what they have created through language, drawing, and writing. They are more willing to read and explore books about the topics they are investigating through building. Many children have had the benefit of rich literacy experiences prior to entering school, but many have not. Often, this is because they have a home language other than English or have not had exposure to books and other print material. What is important to understand, however, is that all young children bring a great deal of knowledge and experience about their world, which they are able to eagerly express through their block building. Although it has been shown that dramatic play centers are one of the best places for children to practice their language skills, a study by Rebecca Isbell and Shirley Raines showed that young children's language during block play actually elicited

more frequent and higher-quality oral language (Wellhousen and Kieff 2001). Teacher observations throughout this book also reveal that young children use more sophisticated language and vocabulary during their block play than they do during targeted small-group literacy lessons or during informal teacher-child conversations.

Using a block during play to represent another object helps prepare young children to understand the abstract symbols used in reading and writing. Drawing, particularly for children who have had limited experiences with reading and writing, is an especially helpful scaffold in this process. In the next few chapters, there are examples of children verbally sharing with adults and peers what they have constructed. The children then move to drawing and writing about their constructions. To encourage children in her preschool classroom to write and draw, Ms. Nicole showed the children how to create their own journals. The following week, she documented this:

Four-year-old Tuaha started off by making his journal. Tuaha asked me if he could draw in his journal. He sounded out "day 1," which he wrote, and then proceeded to draw a blueprint for a tower. Once the drawing was complete, he then used it to build his tower out of blocks.

When he was done with his work, Tuaha asked if he could save the tower. Tuaha independently wrote on a page in his journal, "please save" using invented spelling. The next day, he said he needed to add a door to the tower. So he first added it to the blueprint and then added it to his structure. He continued the same process the following day when he added a basement. Tuaha continued to work on the same tower for a one-week span. His journaling showed his ability to apply drawing and writing for a purpose during play.

Addressing the Physical Needs of Children

> Children are going to class with bodies that are less prepared to learn than ever before. With sensory systems not quite working right, they are asked to sit and pay attention. Children naturally start fidgeting in order to get the movement their body so desperately needs and is not getting enough of to "turn their brain on." What happens when the children start fidgeting? We ask them to sit still and pay attention; therefore, their brain goes back to "sleep."
>
> **Angela Hanscom, "Why So Many Kids Can't Sit Still in School Today"**

Angela Hanscom, the pediatric occupational therapist quoted above, and others are seeing and treating more young children with attention difficulties, visual-spatial problems, sensory and vestibular balance issues, and underdeveloped muscles. These diagnoses are having an impact on children's abilities to maintain attention, develop visual-spatial skills, hold a pencil, and manipulate scissors, and are leading to a host of other problems that interfere with daily learning. Hanscom recommends that children spend time outdoors every day to move their bodies and

to exercise their large muscles. What better way to wake up young brains and bodies than to take engaging materials like blocks and other building materials outdoors? Chapter 3 provides suggestions for doing just that.

For those highly kinesthetic children who need to move when the outdoor options are not available, build life-size structures with them that they can crawl or move through, be inside, stand or walk on, or somehow physically interact with. Giving young children materials to manipulate and physically handle helps build muscle memory, cementing concepts in children's minds (Miller 2004).

Building Twenty-First-Century Skills

> The future belongs to a very different kind of person with a very different kind of mind—creators and empathizers, pattern recognizers and meaning makers. These people—artists, inventors, designers, storytellers, caregivers, consolers, big picture thinkers—will now reap society's richest rewards and share its greatest joys.
>
> **Daniel Pink,** *A Whole New Mind*

Many different terms are used to describe twenty-first-century skills: "noncognitive" skills, social and emotional skills, dispositions, character, and life skills. Given that brain research has shown social and emotional skills to be directly connected to cognitive skills in young children, a more inclusive term seems to be necessary.

In early childhood, we refer to the twenty-first-century skills as children's "approaches toward learning," which was originally defined by the National Education Goals Panel as one of five dimensions of school readiness for early learners, along with physical development, social and emotional development, language development, and cognition. School readiness includes young children's ability to tackle and persist at challenging or frustrating tasks, follow directions, take risks, make and learn from mistakes, and work as a part of a group. Approaches to learning, such as demonstrating initiative and persistence, are behaviors and attitudes that show how children learn, not just what they learn (Hyson 2008). Other twenty-first-century skills include creativity and innovation, critical thinking, problem solving, and communication and collaboration.

Young children develop these skills by engaging in learning experiences through play that strengthens cognitive capacities such as paying attention, remembering rules, and inhibiting impulses to achieve a larger goal (Hyson 2008; Tomlinson and Hyson 2012). The way a child approaches learning is a strong predictor of his later success in school. One study showed that young children with higher levels of attentiveness, task persistence, eagerness to learn, learning independence, flexibility, and organizational skills generally did better in literacy and math at the end of the kindergarten school year and the beginning of their first-grade year (Conn-Powers 2006).

You will find many examples in this book of children learning task persistence and problem solving, such as Ms. Spadola's wood construction study featured in chapter 5. She found that children were able to stay focused when provided with the time, materials, and encouragement to solve problems that arose as they worked: "As part of my research for a class I was taking, I tracked the amount of time children stayed focused while at the wood construction center as well as their persistence and problem solving. I noticed that children who usually weren't motivated were now highly focused and engaged, especially one child who had difficulty transitioning to school in the morning."

Encouraging Creativity and Aesthetic Awareness

> Play-based education in preschool and kindergarten gives children a chance to develop their creativity in balanced ways. It supports the overall healthy development of children and prepares them for the 21st century workplace where creativity is highly valued.
> **Joan Almon, "It's Playtime!"**

Despite the recognition of creativity and innovation as important approaches to learning in the twenty-first century, in our schools creativity is seldom given weight equal to skills such as persistence and self-regulation. Howard Gardner, best known for his theory of multiple intelligences and studies on creativity, describes the creative individual as one who solves problems, makes products, raises questions, poses new ideas, and "thinks outside the box." To support young children's creativity, Gardner says, we need to give them time for thinking and reflection, to focus on their strengths and not worry so much about their weaknesses. Studies show highly creative children can often be challenging and difficult and may have trouble making friends; they may also require more adult support in developing their social skills and seeing defeat as a learning opportunity. We often tell children that their creative expressions or ideas are "great," but we need to help them get better by stretching their thinking and by posing new challenges (Gardner 2010).

For example, if children are frustrated when trying to draw their block structures, you might help them break the task into steps. "What part would you like to start with first?" "What shape do you see?" Without drawing for the child, encourage her efforts and acknowledge that she will get better if she takes her time and keeps trying.

Many adults misunderstand how to support creativity, thinking it means that children are supposed to be totally free and unstructured, that creativity only happens during art, or that only certain people are creative. But creativity can be an important component of every endeavor—math, science, cooking, gardening, and block play—and every child has tremendous creative capacities. Although young children's creative process may begin with play, it involves critical thinking as well as imaginative insight and fresh ideas, many of which develop in collaboration with other children's ideas, especially when they are engaged in a meaningful, in-depth project. The Reggio schools offer exceptional examples of this blend of creativity and deep thinking. They show how important it is to nurture children's new ideas and perspectives, but they also teach children to question their thinking to see if their ideas or theories make sense.

As a young art education student steeped in the ideas of Viktor Lowenfeld, I was excited to learn about the relatively new field of creative, mental, and aesthetic

development. Lowenfeld was known for defining the stages of children's creative self-expression (scribbling, preschematic drawing, schematic drawing, and so on), but he promoted the idea of creativity as being strongly linked to both cognitive and emotional development and insisted that creative development could not be separated from aesthetic development in young children. Lowenfeld defined aesthetics as "being the means of organizing thinking, feeling, and perceiving into an expression that communicates these thoughts and feelings to someone else" (Lowenfeld and Brittain 1970, 31). Like Lilian Katz, he warned against the "anything goes" method of teaching as well as the more authoritarian, teacher-directed methods that included workbooks and coloring sheets. My early indoctrination in this philosophy explains why I am so disappointed with the new fad in adult and child coloring books that are advertised as promoting creativity. They may be great for disconnecting from a stressful world, but there is very little creativity involved in coloring in the lines!

In observing children engaged in creative block play, it becomes clear that as young children manipulate and arrange objects in their constructions, there is a natural attention to organizing them in a beautiful, harmonious design. Children

aren't typically given enough time and adult encouragement to develop aesthetic appreciation, which Lowenfeld felt was essential to human growth. Although Lowenfeld was primarily interested in creative and aesthetic growth through the visual arts, he felt that it should become a major goal in all of education. "To enhance children's intellectual, physical, and emotional experiences, we must turn our attention to learning more about elements of aesthetics and design from other professions. Architects, interior designers, gardeners, artists, and even chefs use aesthetic elements to create inviting, positive experiences for people" (Curtis and Carter 2015, 37).

If Lowenfeld had met Loris Malaguzzi, the founder of the Reggio Emilia schools, known for their focus on creativity, they would have had a wonderful conversation about creativity and how it can be nurtured in young children.

They might have agreed on this point: "Communication puts you in relationship with others—through writing, art, video, speech, mass media. . . . When children learn to draw, it aids in communication, fostering thinking and imagination" (Malaguzzi 1993c).

One way to teach creativity is to encourage divergent thinking through visual thinking. This is why good science teachers, for example, often encourage students to represent their observations or understanding of concepts in drawings. It's important to help children connect with a particular medium or set of materials or processes that excites them. When young children find things they are good at, they tend to get better at everything else as well, because their confidence is up and their attitude is positive toward learning. In addition, it is important to give children many opportunities to collaborate, exchange, and build on each other's ideas, take risks, and problem solve in small-group work and play settings.

Promoting drawing as a means of communication and reflection is something explored in greater detail in chapters 3 and 4, but the manipulation of blocks and open-ended materials as a form of creative expression is also a powerful means of communication for young children.

Strengthening Spatial Ability through STEAM

> Spatial literacy is a significant part of nearly every discipline. It is essential for science, technology, engineering, and mathematics as well as many other professions such as art and graphic design. It is important to promote this emphasis early in life in the context of what children are doing by integrating spatial learning into a variety of subject matter.
>
> **Mary Jo Pollman,** *Blocks and Beyond*

With the national focus now on STEM (science, technology, engineering, and mathematics—or STEAM, which includes the arts), it makes sense to introduce foundational concepts in these content areas through block play in early childhood programs with concrete experiences and investigations that promote problem-solving skills and improve understanding of more abstract concepts. In fact, Piaget concluded that young children could not be taught mathematical understandings through verbal instruction but required hands-on interaction with many kinds of materials. Blocks allow children to "invent their knowledge through manipulation" (Hirsch 1996, 40).

Earlier in my career, I had the opportunity to work with preschool teachers in school districts throughout the state as the early childhood specialist for the

Math Science Partnership at Rutgers University, funded by the National Science Foundation. During this time, I worked with science specialists Jeffrey Winokur, Karen Worth, and Ingrid Chalufour, using their Young Scientist Series on *Building Structures with Young Children* to provide professional development for teachers (Chalufour and Worth 2004). The documentation we collected from early childhood classrooms throughout the state convinced me of the power of block play in helping children learn math and science. Teachers intentionally planned experiences with blocks to help young children learn concepts such as balance and stability, but even more importantly, they assisted children in learning the cycle of inquiry that included engaging in open exploration with blocks, asking questions, clarifying those questions during more focused explorations, recording observations, reflecting on the experience, and drawing conclusions or formulating new ideas and theories. This process can be applied to all areas of learning.

The photograph below shows three- and four-year-old children building a city with unit blocks. The children were interested in the concept of city and thus selected images of cities on the Internet, which were printed and projected in the construction area. The exploration provided many mathematical applications.

This child is thinking about size, scale, and measurement.

Although much has been written about the science and math concepts that young children can learn through blocks (Chalufour and Worth 2004; Dauksas and White 2014; Hirsch 1996; Newburger and Vaughan 2006; Newcombe 2010; Pollman 2010; Tunks 2009; Wellhousen and Kieff 2001), spatial ability typically receives little attention even though current research shows that having good spatial skills strongly predicts children's future achievement in the STEM subjects (Lubinski 2013; Uttal et al. 2013). Cognitive psychologists sometimes refer to spatial ability as the "orphan ability" because it so often goes undetected (Quenqua 2013).

In his theory of multiple intelligences, Howard Gardner (1983) identified visual-spatial intelligence as the ability to think in three dimensions using mental imagery, spatial reasoning, image manipulation, graphic skills, and active imagination. This unique intelligence can be distinguished from other forms of intelligence, such as verbal-linguistic. Words are only one way of communicating. It's not unusual for young children's visual-spatial work to communicate their knowledge of something before they have the ability to verbalize it (Miller 2004). Albert Einstein was known to process information primarily in images, rather than in written words or spoken language (Newcombe 2010), and many children with language disabilities appear to have significant strengths in visual-spatial intelligence (Miller 2004).

Spatial ability is important in our everyday life, as we follow a GPS map or navigate a building so that we don't get lost. But today it is becoming even more critical in fields such as engineering, medicine, and the arts, especially with the increasing use of technology. For example, a surgeon needs to know how to interpret a three-dimensional computer model to perform a delicate surgical procedure, and an engineer or animator needs to be proficient in designing a three-dimensional model using computer graphics. Spatial thinking is not a substitute for verbal or mathematical thinking, however. Those who succeed in STEM careers tend to be very good at all three kinds of thinking—verbal, mathematical, and spatial (Newcombe 2010).

Mark Tompkins (1991) describes the block area of a classroom as the laboratory for spatial thinking, since children encounter and experiment with many spatial concepts and vocabulary when they construct with blocks. Nora Newcombe (2010) has shown spatial language to be a powerful tool for spatial learning when adults give spatial relations a name such as "next to" or "under." Chapter 4 will provide examples of how teachers support children's language, writing, and mathematical skills with many opportunities to strengthen spatial abilities. At this age, young children need the sensory and visual experiences of solid, three-dimensional objects such as blocks that will aid in future applications using technology. The studies stress that even college engineering students should have access to concrete, hands-on materials to develop spatial skills. Materials they can both touch and see stimulate the "perceiving" portion of their brain more than models they see or manipulate on computer screens (Sorby 1999).

In the literature on spatial ability, a wide range of terms, such as "visual-spatial intelligence," "spatial literacy," "spatial visualization," "spatial learning," and "visual-spatial skills," are used to describe different aspects of spatial thinking (Dauksas and White 2014; Gardner 1983; Golbeck 2005; Miller 2004; Newcombe 2010; Pollman 2010; Tompkins 1991). Understanding a few of the basic terms used as children work with shapes and blocks will provide additional guidance in helping to develop children's spatial ability.

Mental Rotation

Mental rotation is the ability to mentally manipulate two-dimensional and three-dimensional objects. In mathematics, sliding, flipping, or turning shapes is called transformation. Having experiences in manipulating blocks lays the foundation for young children to be able to mentally rotate objects (Dauksas and White 2014).

Rotation

A turn is a rotation. As children play with tangrams (a tangram is a set of seven geometric shapes—five triangles, a square, and a parallelogram—that form a square or that can also be used to create an infinite number of other shapes by rotating the shapes), they must use all the shapes by turning them so that they create a square or the desired shape.

Reflection

When children create symmetrical patterns, they place shapes on each side of a mirror line to create "mirror images." Straws, strips of paper, or other objects can be used to represent the mirror line.

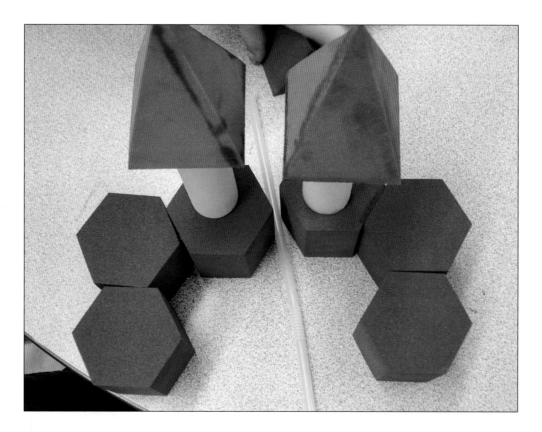

Translation

Sliding or moving a shape without rotating or flipping is a translation. For young children, this would start with stacking shapes on top of one another or placing them parallel to one another.

Part-Whole Integration

Part-whole integration is the ability to know how parts fit together to form a whole. Examples include putting a puzzle together, using one unit block over and over again to create a structure, or organizing a variety of shapes into a completed design. Part-whole integration can also include the ability to take something apart and put it back together again (Golbeck 2005).

Tessellation

A tessellation is created when a shape is repeated over and over again, covering an area, without any spaces between the shapes. Below are examples of tessellations of triangles and squares. Young children can be invited to make patterns like these with unit blocks (Hirsch 1996).

Taking Different Perspectives

The ability to visualize things from different perspectives is another type of spatial thinking. Giving young children experiences in observing people, places, and things from different spatial viewpoints, such as a bird's-eye view from above looking down or inside looking out, helps to build this ability.

Children can view the world from many different perspectives: in the reflection of mirrors, from high places, and through special observation stands with binoculars. A block construction will look very different from above than it does from ground level. The opportunity to practice examining these different points of view in two-dimensional photographs and by moving the body in three-dimensional space will strengthen this ability.

> Spatial awareness begins with children becoming aware of their bodies. An awareness of space outside of the body involves comprehending directions (e.g., left and right, up and down), understanding the projection of oneself in space, and judging the distances between the objects.
> **Mary Jo Pollman,** *Blocks and Beyond*

Representation (Visual Analogies or Creative Representation)

The ability to represent one object to mean another object or place, as in a map, drawing, or construction, and the ability to interpret spatial relations in drawings, pictures, and photographs is explained in more depth in chapters 3 and 4, but it is important to include here. When children are given opportunities to draw their three-dimensional structures from careful observation, as Steven did in these photos, it significantly strengthens their visual-spatial skills (Sorby 1999).

Young children demonstrate a more detailed understanding of space when drawing what they have actually observed, as Tuaha did in his drawing. When children draw what they see, they will remember it, which reinforces visual-spatial memory skills.

You will often find young children building entire cityscapes, which sets the stage for later mapping skills and using blocks to represent other objects, such as phones, couches, beds, tables, and vehicles.

Building and constructing allow children to translate abstract images in their mind or imagination and creatively turn these images into concrete objects. It helps them foster problem-solving skills and develop divergent thinking.

Lisa Daly and Miriam Beloglovsky, *Loose Parts: Inspiring Play in Young Children*

Spatial Relationships, Spatial Awareness, Spatial Orientation

Other important spatial skills for young children to develop include the ability to coordinate use of space, such as knowing how many objects might fit in an enclosure or bucket, and visual-motor skills and eye-hand coordination, such as orienting their bodies in space or building in three dimensions. Experiencing and describing positions, directions, and distances while building also strengthen the development of spatial skills.

Did you know?

- Visual learners are children with high visual-spatial intelligence who think in pictures and images. They are keen observers of the world around them, noticing subtleties and details that most of us miss. They also tend to have an excellent awareness of space and the orientation of their bodies to others (Miller 2004).
- Spatially smart children are good with puzzles, blocks, and other construction toys because they can visualize where a piece might go by mentally manipulating it. These children can also translate concepts from a two-dimensional piece of paper to the three-dimensional world.
- Research indicates that if young children are able to visualize, rotate, and manipulate objects, they have a much greater chance for success in math, especially geometry (Miller 2004).
- Spatial abilities improve as children become more involved with tasks such as model building, working with three-dimensional objects such as blocks and replica buildings, and solving spatial visualization problems (Miller 2004).
- Because visual-spatial learning is seldom addressed in school, young children who have this skill often suffer when their strengths are not supported (Miller 2004).
- Adults with strong visual-spatial skills generally make good architects, photographers, surgeons, pilots, artists, and computer programmers and animators, to name a few occupations (Miller 2004).
- The underrepresentation of women in math, science, technology, and engineering fields could be related to the types of materials that girls are encouraged to play with in early childhood. This makes it essential to encourage play with materials such as blocks, manipulatives, puzzles, and balls to enhance spatial skill development in all children (Pollman 2010).
- It is easy to take advantage of everyday experiences to practice spatial thinking, such as deciding how many blocks will fit into a bin; playing with puzzles, tangrams, and construction games; using maps; and trying out photography (Dewar 2011–12; Newcombe 2010).

You will see from the examples in the next four chapters that young children learn best when they can observe and manipulate real objects, such as blocks and other construction materials, use their previous experiences, engage in language that describes the spatial world, and practice observational drawing as a way to develop spatial skills and strengthen confidence in their unique abilities.

Preparing the Environment for Block Play

> The pleasure of learning, creating, discovering and being together occurs in a physical space. For young children this living happens many hours a day in an early childhood center or school. When a location and its inhabitants can offer children opportunities to create narratives from experience, the children are able to define and redefine themselves. A school becomes a place where there is recognition and a sense of well being within a community of learners.
>
> **Ohio Voices for Learning, "Where Ideas Learn to Fly"**

AN INVITING PLACE FOR ALL TO LEARN AND CREATE

Many years ago I was a novice preschool director fresh out of the classroom and looking for inspiration as my staff and I worked toward NAEYC accreditation. I attended hundreds of workshops, collected more handouts than I could ever read, and purchased books on every imaginable early childhood topic to guide me. Early on in my role as director, I was fortunate to attend symposiums by early childhood educators, including Loris Malaguzzi from Reggio Emilia, and was later able to visit the renowned Reggio Emilia preschools in Italy. During that time, I also attended several workshops by Margie Carter and Deb Curtis and read their book *Designs for Living and Learning: Transforming Early Childhood Environments* and, later in my career, accompanied Margie on a tour of preschools in Auckland, New Zealand.

My lens for looking at early childhood classroom environments was permanently transformed by these experiences, and my eyes opened wide to a new understanding of the Reggio term for the environment as the "third teacher," because the classroom environment is as important as the adults and children in the classroom. When young children are given aesthetically beautiful, clean, safe, well-organized, and culturally friendly environments in which to learn, their senses are stimulated and their feelings of security and belonging are heightened.

When I visit an early childhood classroom, I notice how the environment helps shape relationships and support young children's individual interests and rhythms. I look at the unspoken messages when I enter a classroom:

Who lives and works in this room? Where do I see the identities and learn more about the adults, children, and families that make up this particular classroom community? Do the displays and materials in the room reflect the languages, interests, and values of the classroom community and the wider community as well? Is there evidence that families make meaningful contributions here?

How welcoming does this classroom feel? Are children, families, and visitors warmly greeted? Is the classroom comfortable, bright, and clean, or does it have a more institutional feel? Is there a buzz of excitement and joy in the room?

What kind of learning happens here? Do displays document children's experiences, ideas, and investigations and highlight their authentic, original work? Do children have choices in what they can do, and are they fully engaged in work that has meaning and is of interest to them? Are there places where children can work over extended periods of time without interruption?

What open-ended materials are available to children? Do they provoke a sense of magic and wonder and invite intellectual investment?

As you reflect on the messages that your classroom environment communicates, think about how you can transform your block area by making a few simple adjustments.

Getting Started

First decide where to place the block area, what to put in it, and when to schedule time for block play. Dedicating a sufficient amount of time for children to choose block play—at least forty-five to sixty uninterrupted minutes each day—allows children time to become more deeply engaged in their building and to develop into more experienced builders. If there is not enough time during the day to participate in block play, children may spend most of their time taking materials out and cleaning them up again, which can be frustrating.

The block area should be at least a third of the floor space in your classroom and located in an area away from heavy traffic (Hirsch 1996). If you are lucky enough to have a large classroom, this will allow a small group of children enough space to build elaborate structures and to add to them over time if they are allowed to leave them up. In a smaller classroom, the block area can double as a meeting area, nap area, or large-motor area, but it will mean that blocks will have to be put away after center time is over, and fewer children will be able to build at the same time. If space is at a premium in your program, look around to see if anything can be moved out of the classroom. Sometimes removing extra tables or an unused teacher's desk frees up sufficient space. You can also stretch your space and allow children to move their bodies even more by giving children access to large hollow blocks outdoors.

A wide range of surfaces is available for building. Low-pile carpets or flat hardwood or linoleum floors work well for building on the floor. Some classrooms have raised platforms for building, giving children a protected space with less chance of having constructions accidentally knocked over by passersby.

Provide protected floor space located in the corner of the classroom.

To minimize competition, it is important to provide sufficient space and an adequate number of blocks. Even more importantly, adults help keep children safe by setting up expectations for building behaviors early on and giving children supports and time to practice following the rules (Tunks 2013). Tunks suggests that you keep the guidelines for building simple:

- Blocks are for building.
- Keep blocks in the construction zone.
- Unbuild your own construction only.

Ms. Nicole makes this observation about the four- and five-year-old children who are new to using the block area: "I noticed that Steven and Lucian were two children who needed consistent support from me and my assistant to use the block materials appropriately in order to enhance their learning. We used guided discovery and modeling, and provided verbal and visual cues to promote self-regulation while these boys learned how to use the blocks."

Choosing Blocks

Look through any early childhood supply catalog and you will be dazzled by the wide variety of blocks offered for classroom and home use. When you are selecting blocks, consider how they might stimulate young children's thinking, support their creativity, encourage exploration, and respond to their interests. You will want to steer clear of decorative blocks that leave little to the imagination, and choose blocks that offer more open-ended possibilities. Bamboo, nature blocks, tree blocks, and other natural blocks offer aesthetically pleasing sensory qualities. This book will mainly feature unit blocks, rather than tabletop blocks, because young children need to move their whole bodies during building and should not be expected to sit at tables for extended periods of time (Hirsch 1996). Tabletop shapes and blocks offer many benefits for children who are ready for them, and a few are featured here.

Unit Blocks

Unit blocks were first introduced by Caroline Pratt in the United States in the early 19th century. Pratt was directly inspired by the blocks created by German educator/mathematician/architect Frederick Froebel, known as the "father of kindergarten," and his approach to block play (Hirsch 1996, Pollman 2010). Unit blocks are usually rectangular, made of wood, and measure about $5 \times 1 \times 2\frac{1}{2}$ inches. They come in sets with half, double, and quadruple units, although additional shapes are available.

Large Hollow Blocks

These large wooden blocks are made from natural or painted wood and are excellent for making child-sized structures. Chapters 4 and 5 feature constructions made with hollow blocks.

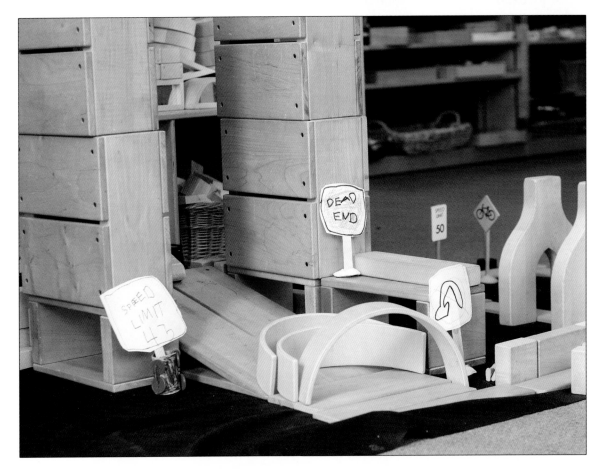

Cardboard Blocks

Other blocks that are good for building on the floor include lightweight, colored cardboard blocks also used for making child-sized structures or stacking in towers.

Foam Building Blocks

Lightweight, dense foam blocks come in a natural wood look and in colors with the same scale and dimensions of unit blocks but at a lower cost. Young children seem to find the foam blocks easy to grip, making them a good choice for children with physical disabilities.

Designer Blocks

These are hardwood blocks in rainbow colors that include three-dimensional squares, rectangles, triangles, and half circles. Designer blocks offer similar benefits to unit blocks for young children, including building inquiry skills, imagination, socialization, and language development through block play, as in this scene from Ms. Nicole's class.

> Adriana: I make houses. Now I need a triangle to make a seesaw.

As she placed the longer block on the triangle, Adriana realized that it would not stay balanced and added the wooden spools. After adding the spools, she said she needed something heavy to make it go down.

> Adriana: I think these will be heavy.

Eventually Diana and Adriana began playing together as each of them added blocks and used verbal exchanges to communicate their ideas. Then the design of their building structure became more detailed and advanced. Diana moved to a different area of the carpet and began to build her own structure as Adriana continued to work on the original. This allowed each child to express her imagination and her thought process in more detail.

Structural Planks

Structural planks are wooden blocks (such as Kapla and Keva planks) that have identical pieces approximately 5 × ½ inch and can be used either on the floor or as tabletop blocks. Dr. Drew's Discovery Blocks include sets of planks, cubes, and blocks.

Connecting Blocks

In addition to the familiar Legos, Duplos, Bristle Blocks, and other colored blocks, children can also construct with straws and connectors and translucent magnetic blocks. HighRise Building Sets are wooden, slotted panels children can connect to create open-ended structures. Interlocking construction materials offer young children different experiences than blocks because they will stay in place when connected, unlike other types of unit blocks that depend on careful balancing to stay in place.

Tabletop Blocks and Shapes

When young children are developmentally ready to sit at a table, there are many three- and two-dimensional shaped blocks that are good for developing fine-motor, mathematical, and problem-solving skills. Children can create interesting designs and structures using architectural unit blocks, mini unit blocks, wood scraps, and other small blocks and shapes. They are also attracted to manipulating translucent materials on a light table.

Organizing the Block Area

Remember that the learning environment is the "third teacher" in an early childhood program. The environment can offer rich learning experiences for young children if you devote the time to organize, store, and care for your building materials and accessories. I often suggest that teachers and providers start with an inventory of the items in the block area to see what they might need to add or eliminate. Often, before anything can be added, the block area needs a decluttering. The fewer overstimulating distractions there are and the more attractive and organized the block area is, the more children will want to focus on the building materials.

Most teachers store unit blocks on shelves specially marked with the outlines of the blocks so children know where to put the blocks after they are done building. Involving the children in organizing the block area will help them feel invested in keeping it orderly.

Chapter 3 is devoted to ideas for accessories to include in your block area, but you will also want to think about how you will store accessories. In addition to storage considerations, you will want to include displays such as nonfiction books; photos, postcards, and posters of buildings and bridges; and other print materials, such as maps. Be sure that your displays reflect the buildings in your community. In the urban classrooms below, children see many tall buildings and bridges every day on the way to and from school. This helps children feel more connected to their communities and inspires their constructions.

Recommended Children's Books on Building

Note: Not all books are geared to three-, four-, and five-year-olds, but those that aren't might have illustrations that children will want to use as a resource.

- *Arches to Zigzags: An Architecture ABC* by Michael J. Crosbie and Steve and Kit Rosenthal
- *At a Construction Site* by Don Kilby
- *Block City* by Robert Louis Stevenson
- *Bridges! Amazing Structures to Design, Build and Test* by Carol A. Johmann and Elizabeth Rieth
- *Build It Up and Knock It Down* by Tom Hunter
- *Building* by Elisha Cooper
- *Building Big* by David Macaulay
- *Building a House* by Byron Barton
- *Building Machines and What They Do* by Derek Radford
- *Building: The Hands-On Approach to Science* by David Glover and Andrew Haslam
- *Construction Trucks* by Jennifer Dussling
- *Construction Zone* by Tana Hoban
- *Dazzling Diggers* by Tony Mitton and Ant Parker
- *Dreaming Up* by Christy Hale
- *How a House Is Built* by Gail Gibbons
- *The Lot at the End of My Block* by Kevin Lewis
- *Machines at Work* by Byron Barton
- *Magic Toolbox* by Mie Araki
- *Roberto: the Insect Architect* by Nina Laden
- *Skyscrapers* by Judith Dupré
- *This Is the House That Jack Built* by Simms Taback
- *The Three Little Javelinas* by Susan Lowell

Children's books on shapes:

- *Changes, Changes* by Pat Hutchins
- *The Cloud Book* by Tomie dePaola
- *Grandfather Tang's Story* by Ann Tompert
- *It Looked Like Spilt Milk* by Charles Shaw
- *Round Trip* by Ann Jonas
- *Sea Shapes* by Suse MacDonald
- *The Shapes of Things* by Dayle Ann Dodds

Caring for Blocks

Some children avoid the block area because they don't like to clean up afterward. One way teachers can help in this process is to develop systems for putting the blocks away. Allowing sufficient time for cleaning up will prevent children from feeling hurried after a pleasant time building. Some teachers develop an assembly line where children pass blocks along to the storage shelves, and others make games out of assigning children specific shapes or quantities to bring to the shelves. Most children are happy to help clean up, even if they were not building with blocks, if there is a classroom culture of cooperation.

Blocks made of hardwood like maple are expensive, but they should last for years if handled with care. Keep them dry, and sand them if they begin to splinter; otherwise they will need little maintenance. The benefits of blocks last a lifetime. Frank Lloyd Wright claimed that one of the influences in his decision to become an architect was the kindergarten blocks he played with as a child (Hirsch 1996, 36). It's hardly surprising that many practicing designers, architects, artists, engineers, mathematicians, and scientists point to their childhood days spent building with blocks and other construction materials as the spark that ignited their career choices!

Meeting ECERS-3 Requirements

If you work in a program that requires your preschool classroom to be assessed using the ECERS-3 (Early Childhood Environment Rating Scale, Third Edition), there is no reason you cannot incorporate the ideas we suggest here for enhancing the block area. You will just need to make sure that you adhere to the following requirements to get credit for scoring:

- There are two types of blocks you must have: unit blocks (but in addition to wood, they can be made of plastic or hard foam) and large hollow blocks (made of wood, cardboard, or plastic) that allow children to build larger structures.
- Accessories required to be stored with the blocks include small people, vehicles (as long as the vehicles do not interfere with building), animals, and other accessories such as road signs, fences, trees, and small buildings.
- When determining the number of blocks needed, consider the developmental abilities of the children in the group. Older children will need more blocks to build more sophisticated structures.
- Blocks should be organized by type (such as wooden unit blocks, plastic unit blocks, and cardboard blocks), but it is not required that the blocks' shapes or sizes be separated in storage. However, to get credit, blocks must be organized by shape/size and type, with labels on the shelves that show images or outlines of the blocks to be stored there (not just the printed words). If accessories are stored in bins, both shelves and containers must have labels.
- If other materials in the block center, such as interlocking construction materials, floor puzzles, carpentry tools, or books on construction, interfere with block play, then credit cannot be given for a special block interest center, unless the space is large enough for three children to build sizable independent structures with blocks at the same time.

- More than one block area may be used during the ECERS-3 observation, such as one indoors and one outdoors, and the combined time at each will be calculated for accessibility.
- Evidence of block building in current display materials can also be considered when scoring.
- To receive the highest score (seven), adults should link written language to children's block play. (For example, write children's comments about what they have built; take photos and write captions; write about shapes children use in structures.) Adults also point out the math concepts that are demonstrated in unit blocks in a way that interests children (such as discussing "more" or "less" and relationships in size or shape).

To score above a 1 on this item, children must be observed building with unit or hollow blocks, and adults must engage with children about their block building. (If children do not play with blocks, or if staff adults do not engage with children around their block play during the observation, this item is an automatic score of 1.)

Exploring Possibilities through Block Play

> You can simultaneously honor childhood and promote a love of learning by adding a wide range of engaging attractions and discoveries to your environment. This is especially effective when you include materials that provoke a sense of mystery and wonder so children become curious and intellectually engaged with objects in the world and what can be learned by manipulating them.
>
> **Deb Curtis and Margie Carter,** *Designs for Living and Learning*

REVISITING THE JOYS OF CHILDHOOD PLAY

In the professional development that I facilitate for early childhood teachers, I have taken cues from the workshops of Margie Carter and Deb Curtis on revisiting childhood memories to remind teachers of what is important in children's learning and play. I ask teachers to close their eyes for a few minutes, to think back to when they were five years old, and to share their childhood memories in their small groups and then with the whole group. You can do a similar activity by asking yourself the following questions:

- Where was your favorite place to play? What places relaxed you most? What places challenged your physical skills, allowing you to take risks?
- Did you play with others or alone? Were the others adults or children?

- Can you describe the play activities that fully engaged you in childhood (the ones you could do for long periods with no sense of time passing)? What was it about these activities that kept your full attention?
- What materials did you most enjoy playing with? Do you remember the scents, sounds, colors, or textures of those materials?

I have been doing this exercise for more than a decade with diverse groups of adults, and I am always fascinated by the similarity of their responses. Almost all of them mention enjoying the freedom of exploring their neighborhoods and communities on foot or by bicycle and being completely unaware of time passing—usually for an entire day! Teachers often describe having had interesting adventures not organized by adults, such as climbing a tree to the very top or building forts in the woods. Many of these adventures involved risk taking, and all of them required a great deal of creative problem solving and collaboration. Quite a few teachers share fond memories of making special dishes or baked goods with a grandparent or playing games with siblings, cousins, or neighbors while their parents played cards or socialized.

Most notable, though, are recollections of the senses: the smell of brand-new crayons, the fragrance of honeysuckle, the sounds of the ocean, the feel of hot sand on bare feet, the shapes and sizes of gathered stones, the sight of a rainbow in the sky, and the earthy scents in the air after a summer storm. Almost no one (except the very youngest) shares memories of plastic or electronic toys, sitting in front of a screen, riding in the car, or going to music lessons or soccer practice. Teachers' most cherished memories almost always include simple and inexpensive pleasures. These memories are usually about spending time with special adults or good friends, about having the freedom to explore without constant adult direction, and about using found or natural items to spark the imagination for creative play.

Once you get reacquainted with the inner joys of childhood play and exploration, you will begin to see endless new possibilities for making the block area of your classroom more attractive, interesting, and challenging. You will see how props and accessories can provide prompts that encourage elaboration of children's ideas and language.

Few of the props and accessories suggested in this book have to be purchased. You can find many of these items in attics and basements, on nature walks, at flea markets, or by requesting them from colleagues, families, and home supply or craft stores. You will need to ensure that all items are safe and clean before repurposing them for the block area, and you will want to be careful not to offer so many accessories that they distract children from building. Remember that it is often better for children's imaginations when they create their own props and accessories from materials, such as recycled plastic containers and lids, carpet or fabric scraps, ribbon, and clothespins, than when children have ready-made materials. You will see a wide variety of props and accessories illustrated in this chapter.

Inspiring Construction with Accessories and Materials
Add Traditional Accessories and Props to the Block Area

road signs and carpet maps

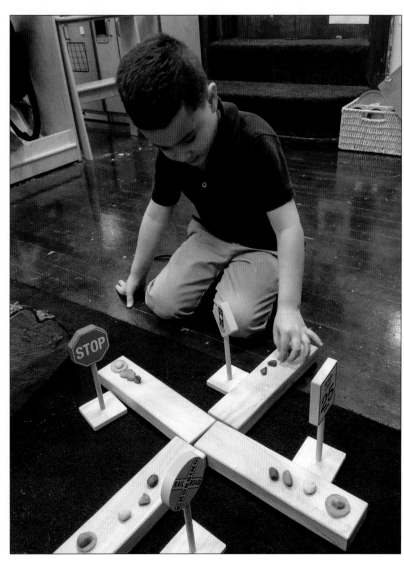

wooden, fabric, or plastic animals and human figures

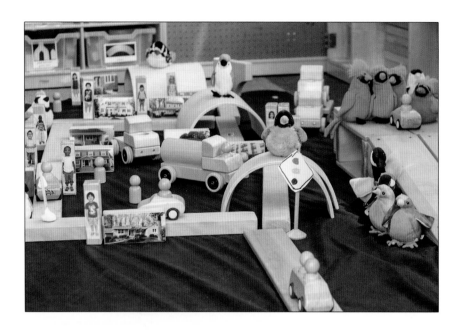

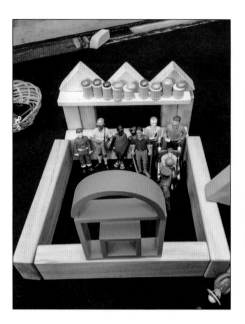

vehicles and ramps

measuring instruments such as tape measures, rulers, and nonstandard measuring instruments

dramatic play items such as dolls and doll furniture, toy food and other kitchen items, construction hats, and so on

additional materials related to children's emerging interests (Encourage children to contribute materials.)

Enhance Construction with Loose Parts

"Loose parts" is the term architect Simon Nicholson coined in the early 1970s to describe open-ended materials that can be used and manipulated in many ways (Daly and Beloglovsky 2015). In the following photos, children offer just a few examples of using loose parts in an early childhood setting.

Ordinary natural and recycled materials of wood and cork become extraordinary additions to children's constructions.

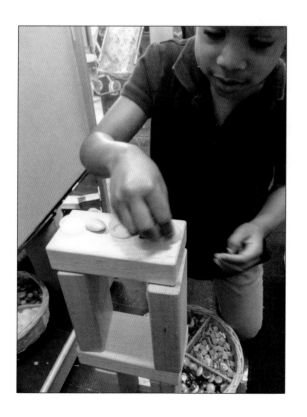

Children can use beads, sea glass, or "jewels" to embellish their constructions. Five-year-old Jayde constructs a building and says, "Okay, I need to build the windows." Then she says, "I need signs."

In their book *Loose Parts,* authors Lisa Daly and Miriam Beloglovsky (2015) say that loose parts such as natural and recycled materials offer unlimited potential for learning in children's functional, symbolic, constructive, and dramatic play. This potential is evident in the following story about Tuaha.

Four-year-old Tuaha was playing independently with a selection of natural materials. When he was done with his creation, he called his peers over in excitement. He explained how he used sea glass to create water. He created a pattern of wooden spools around the water. He explained that this pattern was the sand.

Tuaha said, "Water is blue, and water you can swim in. But this water needs a boat, because the boat brings people back and forth."

Tuaha said, "The people need a bridge." He used the large semicircular tree cookie to make a bridge. He worked on this creation over four days.

Tuaha then asked if he could draw his creation. When he started drawing, he said, "I can't draw the shells. I don't know how." He sat there for a minute, and then he took one shell at a time and traced it and placed it back on his creation.

This story shows how Tuaha used his prior knowledge along with his vivid imagination to create a detailed masterpiece. Using loose parts, he was able to demonstrate his cognitive skills: applying prior knowledge, problem solving, and staying engaged in a task for a long period of time. Tuaha also demonstrated how he writes to convey meaning, along with his letter-sound connection. He was able to create a complex pattern and demonstrate many other mathematical concepts as well.

Nicole Dennis, Paterson, New Jersey

Examples of Loose Parts

Here are a few examples of loose parts you could use with young children:

- natural materials: leaves, shells, corks, seedpods, pinecones, stones, twigs, driftwood, bark, small branches, tree cookies, bamboo segments of various sizes, flower petals, wood scraps
- recycled materials: fur pieces, scarves, artificial flowers and leaves, bottle caps, buttons, fabric and carpet pieces, yarn, hardware, cardboard tubes, ceramic tiles, small boxes, telephone wire, rope, Popsicle sticks, keys

According to Daly and Beloglovsky, using loose parts promotes active learning, deepens critical and creative thinking, and encourages flexibility. They explain, "Children of all ages, abilities, skill levels, and genders can use loose parts successfully. Because there's no right or wrong way to work with them, all children can achieve competence, build on existing strengths, and feel successful and independent" while using them (2015, 14). Loose parts support play for children of all socioeconomic and cultural backgrounds.

After years of field research, observations, and interviews, Walter Drew and Baji Rankin (2005) have identified seven key principles for using open-ended materials in early childhood classrooms:

1. Children's spontaneous, creative self-expression increases their sense of competence and well-being now and into adulthood.
2. Children extend and deepen their understanding through multiple hands-on experiences with diverse materials.
3. Children's play with peers supports learning and a growing sense of competence.
4. Children can learn literacy, science, and mathematics joyfully through active play with diverse, open-ended materials.

5. Children learn best in open-ended explorations when teachers help them make connections.
6. Teachers are nourished by observing children's joy and learning.
7. Ongoing self-reflection among teachers in community is needed to support these practices.

Supplement Building Materials with Art Materials, Clipboards for Drawing, and Art Books

Ms. Spadola and Ms. Nicole provide unlined drawing paper and markers so children can draw the structures they've built.

Ms. Nicole provides Melanie with an art book, colored gems, a clipboard, unlined paper, and markers. Melanie is inspired by the book and the gems.

Buildings can be represented through many visual languages: blocks, drawings, line printing, and cut-paper murals.

Supply Writing Materials and Journals

In addition to drawing, children can communicate their ideas through writing. Teachers often start by writing the words children dictate and then offering materials to help children "write" using letter-like forms or letter strings to describe the stories of their constructions. Making a variety of writing tools available in the block area along with building journals, clipboards, and sign-making supplies will encourage more frequent writing for a purpose.

 Five-year-old Ava has an idea. She wants to set out food so the birds can find their house. Her teacher, Ms. Nicole, asks Ava to say more about her idea.

Ava: I'll make it strong like the brick house in The Three Little Pigs, *so they can live safely. I have a bird at my house. He's blue, white, and black. His name is Fluffy. I fix his house so he can live.*

Ms. Nicole: Tell me more.

Ava: He's cute. He eats and drinks. (Then Ava counts out flowers from one to thirty-one, using one-to-one correspondence.)

Ms. Nicole: Why do you need all those flowers by your birdhouse?

Ava: So they don't be hungry.

Ms. Nicole: Why is it important for birds to have a house?

Ava: Because they always fly, and they need to rest so their bodies can get relaxed and their bodies get nice and strong. And so then they can play with other birds.

Ava wrote two poems. This one is called "A Birdy."

> *His name is birdy birdy*
> *Ladder*
> *Climb to the top*
> *Food*
> *Eat eat eat*
> *Water*
> *Drink drink drink*
> *Thirsty no more!*

Children can typically write their own names and other high-frequency words, as Ava demonstrates. Providing children with block journals in which they can record or dictate experiences related to their building helps them chronicle their construction activities. It also helps document children's abilities as writers (Giles and Tunks 2015).

While placing her stones in a spiral, Adriana, age five, observed, "Look, they go around and around, then they stop. It make me dizzy 'cause it goes around and around. I think it looks like a Ferris wheel. Okay, I need to write about it now. I need to get the block journal." Adriana then took out a sheet of paper and began to write. Her teacher, Ms. Nicole, said, "Tell me about what you are writing."

Adriana responded, "Rocks go around the circle and stop." When she was about to write the word "stop," she walked over and picked up the stop sign and said, "This help me spell 'stop.' This in English so my friends can read and Spanish for my daddy."

Nicole Dennis, Paterson, New Jersey

Young dual-language learners like Adriana need play experiences such as block building and journaling to reinforce literacy in both English and their home language. Illustrated books on construction careers and community buildings written in the languages of the children in the classroom make the block area more inviting. So do community and family volunteers who spend time with children in the block area to practice vocabulary and concepts in children's home languages. Adult volunteers can also help children write words in their home languages (Nemeth 2012).

Over the years, the children in Ms. Marianne's class have created how-to books with titles such as the following:

- *Making a Circle with Train Tracks*
- *How to Add a Loop to a Circle Train Track*
- *How to Make a Hideout*
- *How to Make Paper Flowers*
- *How to Be the Paintbrush Washer*
- *How to Make Astronauts*
- *How to Work with K'nex*

At the beginning of each year, I welcome the new children with books and gifts made for them by the previous year's children. In my classes, we have a year-end tradition of leaving a legacy for the next year's "little kids." A few years ago, the children made a book called How to Make Playdough. *It has a recipe for three children to make a batch of playdough. That recipe is what we use throughout the year whenever we need to make a new batch of playdough. I find it creates a fabulous context for reading and mathematics.*

That playdough book turned out to be inspirational for the children in my class last year. They were having trouble with the marble maze, so they made a book called How to Work with Marbles. *To make the marble book, we took step-by-step photos of building a working marble run. The marble book has become the reference text for children's independent play in marbles. If something isn't working, one child or another will usually get the marble book to troubleshoot.*

Also last year, we started to gather together games that the children enjoyed involving paper. We pulled those into a Paper Games *binder with slash-front pockets and page protectors. It lives in the communications center. When the children want to make a puppet, a rocket ship, or a mask, the templates and Lego-like step-by-step illustrations are in the binder to guide them. We also made a binder last year titled* How to Make Recycled Paper.

Given this group of children's eagerness to go to the manuals for information, it was natural that they would be interested in making how-to books to pass on how to do the tricky construction skills they were mastering. Using books to communicate and to learn is a strong goal of mine as a teacher and for these particular children as learners.

Marianne Cane, Englewood Public School District, Englewood, New Jersey

Children build a tunnel ramp using the book they wrote, How to Make a Tunnel Ramp.

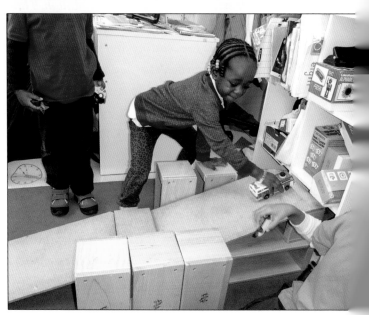

Use Light and Technology to Display or Project Videos or Images

The three-year-old children in Ms. Sarah's class were building in their classroom construction area, which included building platforms of various surfaces and levels. They were driving small toy cars on roads built from blocks and wondered how to get the cars from one level to the next. At this point, the teachers introduced the idea of a drawbridge. The children researched drawbridges on the Internet and found several videos. Here one of those videos is projected in the background as a point of reference for the children as they build. Notice how the children use the projected video of a drawbridge as a reference.

Alison Maher, Boulder Journey School, Boulder, Colorado

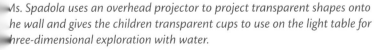

Ms. Spadola uses an overhead projector to project transparent shapes onto the wall and gives the children transparent cups to use on the light table for three-dimensional exploration with water.

Children use erasable markers to trace shapes from a community walk displayed on an interactive whiteboard in Ms. Spadola's class.

Entice Reluctant Children to the Block Area with Materials That Will Attract Their Attention

Some children may be intimidated by boisterous play in the block area. One way to attract these children to play with blocks is to add materials that appeal to them. For example, striking elements such as colorful shapes, pretty fabrics, scarves, artificial flowers, or sparkly jewels may attract children who are drawn to visual beauty.

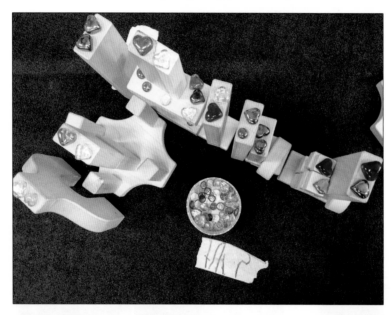

Join Blocks Together from Other Classrooms into a Larger Space

In order to offer the children an opportunity to experience large quantities such as hundreds, we coordinated with all fifteen classrooms of children and teachers to bring their unit blocks to a large common space for several weeks. This required a great deal of cooperation, and it encouraged more elaborate construction.

Alison Maher, Boulder Journey School, Boulder, Colorado

Introduce Nontraditional Materials to the Block Area

mud

sand

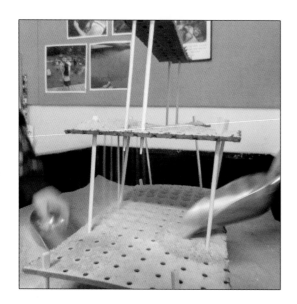

unbreakable mirrors

Ms. Nicole says, "Using a mirror, this child will develop a stronger foundation in understanding angles, height, and perspective."

Extending Construction with Unexpected Materials

Styrofoam balls and wooden dowels or sticks

cardboard boxes

wood shapes and scraps

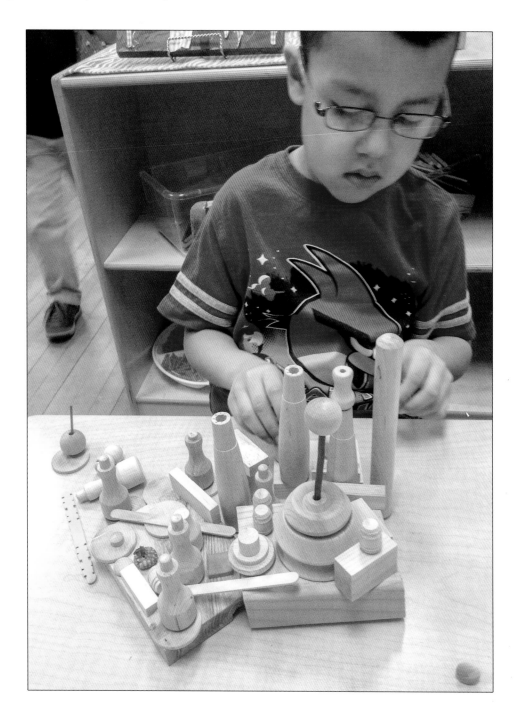

Inviting the Community In and the Children Out

This bridge was created spontaneously by a group of four-year-olds. The teachers observed the children using their knowledge of engineering and design to create the bridge. Later the teachers extended this work by inviting a parent who is an architect to join the children in the construction area and add her knowledge to that of the group. In this series of photos, the engineering and design principles are evident in their work.

Alison Maher, Boulder Journey School, Boulder, Colorado

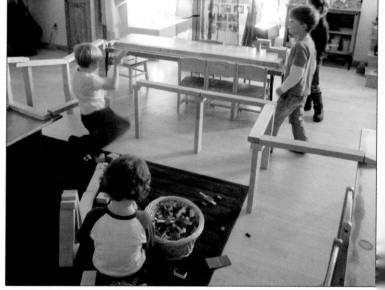

Take Field Trips and Visit Museums

The skyscraper exhibit at the Liberty Science Center in Jersey City, New Jersey, celebrates the tallest architectural wonders of the world, including skyscrapers from the New York City skyline that children can see from the second floor of the center. Although the exhibit is designed for older children, young children can be guided through it to see the structural components of buildings such as columns, beams, and elevators; they can learn about the importance of strong, stable foundations to protect against earthquakes; they can see architectural models of buildings in various design stages; they can explore careers in building design and construction; and they can even create skyscrapers with building blocks.

Although you may not have a museum like this in your backyard, taking field trips in your own community to find architectural treasures, such as covered bridges, old barns, lighthouses, windmills, churches, libraries, and other landmarks, provides inspiration for children's block building. Taking photos and bringing them to post in the block area will help children remember the details of the buildings and structures they visited.

Taking Blocks Outdoors

Start with Small Groups

Children in early childhood settings typically have scheduled time for play outdoors, but what I am suggesting here is that adults take small groups of children outdoors during the day when the playground or other outdoor spaces are typically not being used. For example, Ms. Spadola, a preschool teacher in one district, noticed that the children in her classroom were losing interest in building. She got permission to take a small group of children outdoors for block building and organized their help in bringing the blocks and other accessories outdoors. Ms. Spadola inten-

tionally grouped the children so that they could comfortably collaborate without other students interrupting their play. One of the exciting benefits of being outdoors on a bright, sunny day was that the children started to notice the shadows the sun cast on their three-dimensional constructions. This would not have been possible indoors in a classroom with little natural light.

Create a Woodworking Area for Using Construction Tools

Once children gain confidence in using real construction tools under the guidance of teachers, they can become more independent in building.

The Universal Studio Child Care Center takes advantage of the warm climate in Los Angeles to offer children a well-stocked outdoor woodworking center.

Create a Designated Building Area Stocked with Wooden and Bamboo Blocks

Environmentally friendly, waterproof blocks made from a variety of woods and bamboo are available for outdoor use. Storage units made of exterior-grade, natural or weather-treated wood provide children easy access to the blocks and a convenient place to house the blocks without transporting them to the classroom.

Two of the programs highlighted in this section, Abington Friends School in Jenkintown, Pennsylvania, and the Quarles School in Englewood School District, Englewood, New Jersey, are fortunate to have received funding to build Nature Explore playgrounds, a collaborative program of the nonprofit organizations Arbor Day Foundation and Dimensions Educational Research Foundation. Among the special features of these playgrounds are the natural construction materials and loose parts that not only connect children to the natural world but also provide them with safe and appropriate building opportunities outdoors.

Set Up Balance Beams and Ramps

Tamara Clark of Abington Friends School in Jenkintown, Pennsylvania, explains, "The playground has several different areas for big body movement. In one area, stumps are mounted in a group for jumping. Much discussion went into the placement of the stumps, as the playground is for ages three through almost six years old. This meant that some of the stumps were high enough to be challenging for the older children and too high for some of the younger children to navigate independently. This provided a much-needed physical challenge for all ages. In another area of the playground, we had a Big Building area (sometimes called a Messy Materials Area). The area was equipped with big hollow blocks,

boards, tree branches, loose stumps, sections of bark, and PVC pipes. This area was entirely fueled by the children's imagination. Some days it turned into long, low race cars with seats for everyone. Other days homes were built for people or animals. And sometimes it was just the joy of experimentation. Children learned to work carefully with the long boards and sticks, relishing the hard work of lifting and placing them, exploring the ways that the boards could hold their weight or the ways that the uneven surface made the boards tippy."

Add Natural Materials, Such as Tree Cookies, Branches, and Boards, for Building and Dramatic Play

"In the outdoor block building area," Tamara Clark writes, "we have a bin of cedar wood blocks, a bin of tree blocks, and a bin of tree cookies. Annabel is an expert builder (and the daughter of engineers), and frequently works in the classroom creating complex buildings characterized by symmetry, height, and bridges between levels. She had not worked much with building with small blocks outdoors, preferring instead active games of chase or climbing. On this day, I set up an invitation on the table, balancing one tree cookie on end and arranging a bunch of tree blocks on the table around it. Annabel watched the setup with interest and quickly jumped in to work. She balanced block after block on the tree cookie, carefully finding the balance point for each circle. As she reached her limit, she counted her work, using each block as one unit of measure. Amazingly, her work did not fall once during her careful building. Because the space was used by different classrooms, we would often enter the classroom to find a partial structure left behind by the kindergartners. It was just such a structure that began a days-long exploration of pivot points and balance. A group of children discovered a 'seesaw' that the kindergartners had created with a small log and a board. Two four-year-olds immediately identified it as a seesaw and tried to sit on either side. The board was too short to sit on and slid off the log when they tried. They replaced the board, and this time, one girl stood on the end. She carefully stepped toward the middle, the board shifting slightly under her feet. She tentatively stepped onto the middle, the pivot point, balancing with her whole body tense. She stepped onto the other side,

and the board switched orientation. She triumphantly walked down the slope to the ground. Next her friend tried, and the two continued to test the edges of their balance and control with this simple setup."

Provide Large Blocks or Crates and Accessories for Dramatic Play

Tamara Clark describes, "Near our small water fountain stream, a teacher set up an invitation inspired by a child's distressed observation, 'The bucket has a hole!' Using two large blocks to hold up the leaky bucket, she placed a pot underneath the contraption. From there, Harper spent over an hour carrying cups of water to pour into the leaky bucket and observing the rate of flow of the water into the lower bucket."

Offer Pipes and Tubing for Experimenting with Motion

Tamara Clark explains, "The PVC pipes and ladders are part of a Kodo Kids set but could also be made fairly easily. Because the materials are flexible and open-ended, they allow for many different configurations. We have used them with cars, balls, water, and marbles. The materials themselves invite the children into problem solving and collaboration, and so with very little input from the teachers, the children work to figure out incline, velocity, and how to layer or connect the ramps so that the balls won't jump the track."

Supporting Children during Block Play

> Expert teachers constantly adapt their strategies to the needs and opportunities of the moment. Effective teaching is a constant process of adjustment, judgment, and responding to the energy and engagement of the students.
> **Ken Robinson and Lou Aronica,** *Creative Schools*

THE ROLE OF THE ADULT

The early childhood literature suggests that effective teacher-child interactions have a significant impact on children's early social-emotional development. Teachers who are warm, affectionate, and respectful contribute to children's engagement in school. If the teacher cares, children put forth more effort in their work. When teachers create a classroom environment that is structured with clear, fair, and consistent rules and routines, children are better able to regulate their own behavior. Positive interactions also support the development of children's approaches to learning skills, including attention, persistence, and frustration tolerance—skills that are linked to better early learning outcomes. When teachers are responsive to children and respect their autonomy, they contribute not only to children's language and literacy development but also to their ability to hold information in memory. In addition, when teachers provide instructional supports for children, including teaching concepts, giving quality feedback, and modeling language, children progress academically (Dombro, Jablon, and Stetson 2011; Society for Research in Child Development 2013; Teachstone/CLASS 2014).

As children explore with blocks, teachers build on the positive relations they have established with each child and take on a more challenging role in supporting children's developing block play. This happens when teachers observe and document block play, thereby becoming more familiar with the needs and interests of the children and where they are in their stage of block play. The best instructional strategy to use depends on these careful observations but might include words of encouragement, targeted feedback, modeling, offering assistance, providing information, and giving directions (Gullo 2006).

Providing Time for Open Exploration with Blocks

When I was a college student taking my very first watercolor course, I was fortunate to have a professor who understood that I needed time to play with the materials to see what they could do. This opportunity alleviated some of my anxiety about having no prior experience with watercolors, and it helped me be more open to learning techniques when I was ready.

Likewise, some children may never have played with blocks before or may have had only limited exposure to different types of blocks. These children will need ample time to get to know blocks through open exploration or unstructured play. Setting up the block area and establishing rules, as explained in chapter 2, will ensure a more successful block-building experience for the novice. When children are peacefully engaged in open exploration with blocks, it is tempting to move on to other areas of the room where children might need your attention. But moving children to higher levels of creative block play requires that you devote some time in the block area gathering information through observation and documentation.

Observing and Documenting Children's Building

Becoming more attuned to children's block play requires practice in careful listening, supported by observational notes and photos, that will reveal what children are building, who they are playing with, what problems they are encountering, what they are learning about the properties of blocks, what interests they express during building, and other valuable clues to what and how children are learning. Your observations and notes will help you respond to each child individually, if not on the spot, perhaps later when you have had a chance to revisit your notes. The teachers featured in this chapter have had considerable practice in observation and documentation and share their strategies for developing this skill.

Because not all three-, four-, and five-year-olds are at the same stage of development with regard to block play, it is important to know where children are developmentally in their block play. In 1933, child development researcher Harriet Johnson identified seven stages of block play that all children pass through regardless of when they are introduced to blocks (Hirsch 1996, 142). The following list describes these stages.

Understand the Stages of Block Play

Stage 1: Very young children primarily carry blocks from one place to another without using the blocks for construction.

Stage 2: Preschool- and kindergarten-age children put blocks side by side in rows or stack them in repetitive patterns.

Stage 3: Children begin bridging by placing two blocks with a space between them, connected by a third block.

Stage 4: As children gain experience with blocks, they begin to create enclosures, or place blocks together in such a way that they enclose a space. This is not as easy for children as it may seem. Building an enclosure may require repeated attempts and concentrated problem solving. Children may design enclosures for a purpose, such as creating a holding place for animal or people figures.

Stage 5: As children grow older and more experienced, their block building becomes more sophisticated and imaginative. They create more elaborate designs with noticeable patterning and balance, using a larger number and variety of blocks.

Stage 6: Children begin to name structures in their dramatic play. Children may have named structures prior to this stage, but now their words are more closely related to the functions of the buildings.

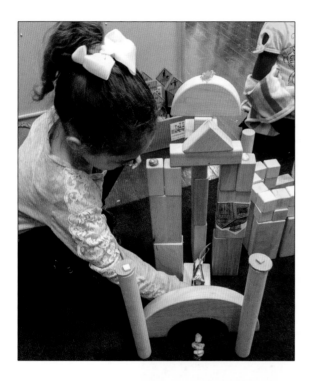

Five-year-old Maribel points to the rocks leading up to her structure and tells her teacher that they are the little stairs that birds can walk on to get the food inside the house.

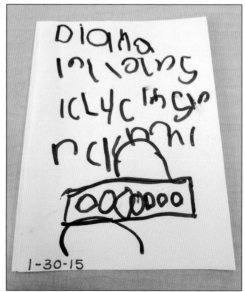

Four-year-old Diana describes the bird's nest she has built and embellished with "diamonds and flowers." Like Maribel, Diana has added rocks in front for birds to "jump on." She points to where the birds can find food in her structure.

Stage 7: Children begin to reproduce or symbolize actual structures they know.

A kindergartner constructs a train museum during a transportation unit.

Listen to Learn, Inform, and Assess

> Listening [is] welcoming and being open to differences, recognizing the value of the other's point of view and interpretation. Listening is an active verb that involves interpretation, giving meaning to the message and value to those who offer it.
>
> **Carlina Rinaldi,** *Making Learning Visible: Children as Individual and Group Learners*

Carlina Rinaldi, a Reggio Emilia pedagogical expert, notes in her "Pedagogy of Listening" that "children cannot bear to be anonymous" (Project Zero and Reggio

Children 2001, 81). Rinaldi emphasizes that by really listening to children, adults can help children make their ideas visible. As you become more accomplished at listening, you will see how incredibly capable, curious, and creative children can be with blocks, and you will gain a deeper appreciation for children's strengths and abilities. You will also develop a greater understanding of the concepts children are building, the theories they are constructing, the questions they are asking, and where they might need more support.

What does it mean to listen carefully to children when they are engaged in block play? You might start with this list of questions to guide your observations:

- What do you notice as children are building?
- What do you notice about children's language during the building process?
- What stories do children tell while they are playing with blocks?
- What themes emerge from children's play with blocks, and how might you build on them?
- What problems arise, what strategies do children use to solve these problems, and how do adults support this problem solving?

Solving Problems

The children in Ms. Nicole's preschool classroom face many challenges. Their urban school district serves mostly low-income families. One-third of the children in Ms. Nicole's class are English-language learners, more than 85 percent of them receive free and reduced lunch, and three children have special needs. Ms. Nicole knows that these children need extra supports in order to be successful. During her classroom's study of buildings in the community, Ms. Nicole gave the children ample time to gain experience with block building. Even so, she noticed that the children were having difficulty playing cooperatively and maintaining friendships because they were constantly arguing over construction materials and accessories.

Children's play was immature, and communication among peers and with me was limited. I realized that I needed to make changes to the block area that would provoke more meaningful play. In the beginning, my role was to observe and note the children's interests and interactions. Sometimes I needed to provide more support for some children through questioning and modeling. With other children, I really could just sit back and watch as the children showed me their independence and self-motivation.

Based on the ideas of Reggio Emilia and on Nicholson's theory of loose parts, I set up the physical environment with rich, open-ended, natural materials like pinecones, shells, rocks, sea glass, marbles, and tree cookies, hoping to encourage children to plan, construct, and document their ideas. I also added wooden spools, wooden dowels, mirrors, tile pieces, gems, plastic spools, paper towel rolls, artificial flowers, birds and nests, animal figures, and nonfiction books to the block area, which already contained wooden unit blocks, tree blocks, rainbow blocks, cardboard blocks, and hollow blocks.

At the same time, I knew I needed to make learning in the block area more authentic, based on the children's interests, and more focused on exploration and discovery with all the senses. I wanted to help the children make plans, ask good questions, test theories, problem solve, and think deeply. When children started collecting natural materials and loose parts outside to add to our discovery area, I heard them ask, "Where did this stick come from?" "Why does that bird fly?" "Why are these rocks on the playground?" They began to use these natural materials to create artwork. That's when I thought it would make sense to add loose parts to the block area in place of store-bought toys.

After adding the new materials, I began to observe and document children during block play and immediately saw a change in the children's building. The children were motivated to plan their play and investigate with their peers. They began discussing problems and exploring new topics and concepts related to their structures. During my observations, the children began to ask to save their structures in order to complete their construction or to show their family members during pickup time. I knew that introducing journaling would give children a way to preserve their work so that they could share it with their families. I modeled how to use the journals and how to think aloud when determining what to build. I noticed a change in how the children began the construction process. The children began to plan their structure before building their construction.

I noticed that children used the natural and open-ended materials I offered in highly creative, flexible, and inventive ways, demonstrating their wide range of abilities and their understanding of social, emotional, language, cognitive, literacy, science, and art concepts. Children were able to use open-ended materials to express themselves. Once I set the stage for play, the children did not require my constant presence but became independent thinkers and problem solvers by making connections to prior knowledge and applying that knowledge to new situations. I also noticed that the colorful and interesting new materials drew the girls into the block play.

In addition to the improvement in children's interactions, the higher level of play, and the increase in communication skills and language, I was especially impressed with the children's imaginative creations. A book by ephemeral artist Andy Goldsworthy was especially powerful in inspiring the children (Goldsworthy 1990).

Here Steven and Adriana are inspired by photos from a book of Andy Goldworthy's art made from natural materials to build block creations using stones and gems and to write for a purpose.

I observed and interacted first, without taking notes, during the beginning of the provocation. Then toward the middle and the end, I recorded conversations that happened as the children worked. I used a still camera, a video camera, and an audio recorder to capture their words and actions. The challenge, I found, was taking notes and keeping up with the children's conversation without missing important dialogue. Next time I would like to record the block area when I am not present, for uninterrupted play and more authentic observation.

The camera allowed me to document each step and document from different perspectives. Using the block journal allowed me to observe how the children viewed their own structures from their perspectives, which I thought was very interesting and important to understanding how they think.

Nicole Dennis, Paterson, New Jersey

Documentation

Ms. Nicole and several of the teachers who contributed to this book included the photos, quotes from children, and descriptive narratives in their district-required assessments. We know that this type of documentation is a more accurate and reliable way to assess what children know than a paper-and-pencil test. Capturing children's works and words by using whatever technologies are available, such as video cameras, digital cameras, tablets, and audio recorders, offers a way to collect documentation over time. This documentation then becomes a valuable record of learning that can be shared with families, giving them new perspectives on their children and better understanding of what their children have learned. To do this effectively, adults must be highly organized and must create systems for collecting the documentation so that every child is included.

Responding with Thoughtful Feedback

Adults sometimes underestimate children's ability to stay engaged in a building project based on the perception that young children have very short attention spans. While that may be true for activities that offer little intellectual challenge or interest, children can stay focused for a surprisingly long time when offered meaningful experiences, provocations for deep thinking, challenges to solve problems, and thoughtful adult feedback.

When teachers talk with me about their involvement in children's block play, they often tell similar stories. They find it challenging to be involved just enough in children's play to support more complex thinking or language without taking over or interfering with the play. The following strategies and examples will guide you in giving specific feedback and support to children as they build.

Ask Open-Ended Questions

Adults can help children sustain attention to their building by asking questions such as the following:

- What part of the building are you adding to here?
- What would be interesting to add?
- I wonder what would happen if . . . ?

Following is one example of open-ended questioning from Ms. Nicole's classroom.

Kaden uses unit blocks to build a hotel he visited with his family.
Ms. Nicole: Can you tell me about your structure?
Kaden: I made a hotel. It's called the Hamilton Inn. It has a roof on it so it
   don't rain on it. Look, I wrote "door."

Adults are often surprised to find that the block area offers a context for dramatic play that the housekeeping area, with its prescribed furnishings and materials, may not. This kind of dramatic play is especially likely when an unexpected material is added to the block area. Children use blocks in creative ways to accommodate their play as they plan what to build, raise questions, solve problems, and decide which roles to play. In addition to the usual roles of baker, receptionist, cashier, and waiter, notice the role of scientist that the preschoolers in the following story play. This scene unfolds in an inquiry-based classroom, where open-ended questions take center stage.

While exploring several abandoned nests, the children decide they want to make new nests for the birds. They wonder if birds would use the nests if they put the nests in trees. They collect twigs and leaves and begin to re-create the nests. Within a few days, their play shifts from making mud nests to making mud. The children start exploring the properties of mud. The teachers realize that this is an opportunity to introduce a new provocation or a starting point for trying something more challenging.

The teachers ask several questions while engaged in conversation with the children the next morning: "What is mud?" "What do you need to make mud?" "Will I always make mud if I just pour dirt and water together?" "If you were going to make mud, what might you want to create with the mud?"

The children say that they are going to be "mudologists," just like when they were "ornithologists" and were learning about birds. Now they are going to change "ologists," because now they want to learn about mud. A teacher asks the children what they want to learn about mud, and they say, "Everything!" When the teacher asks what "everything" means, the following conversation occurs.

> *Child 1: You know, like when you always ask us how something feels. Well, how does mud feel? That's what I want to know.*
> *Teacher: I wonder how it will feel when I touch it with my fingers.*
> *Child 1: Cold, gushy, wet, and muddy, that's how.*
> *Child 2: Don't forget slimy.*
> *Child 3: Well, I already know a lot about mud, but I want to know how it feels when I touch it with my toes!*
> *Child 4: Well, I am still going to be a mudologist and learn everything.*

That morning the children read the picture book Bunny Cakes *by Rosemary Wells. Afterward they have another conversation.*

Child 1: Hey, I have a good idea. Let's make mud pies like Max.

Teacher: What would we need to gather together to make mud pies?

Child 2: Dirt, sticks, cups, buckets, water, and—oh yeah—don't forget measuring cups.

Child 3: Just leave it to us.

Child 4: You know, after we learn this, maybe we can help you make a recipe so everyone can make mud like us.

Child 5: Now that's gonna be a real challenge for everybody.

The children work together in their outdoor mud center. They mix, pour, stir, and dump until they are satisfied with their results. They are determined to mix the right proportions of dirt and water in order to create the perfect mud pie. Their play continues throughout the day. They are quite satisfied with their results. The teachers, however, wonder what will become of their interest the next day; the weather forecast includes high winds and heavy rain.

While the teachers worry about the children losing interest because of the weather, the children come up with a solution.

Child 1: Why can't we just put plastic on the rug like we do for all the other messy things we do in the classroom?

Child 2: Yeah, and we can just use the blocks and the cardboard and make a mud bakery and sell mud pies and earthworm cakes, too.

Child 3: And I will make signs so everybody brings money for the pies.

With each new story the children read, they add more and more to their mud bakery. One day, they read Mud Tacos! *by Mario Lopez and Marissa Lopez Wong.*

Child 1: Hey, I have a new challenge for us. Since we are kind of done making mud cupcakes for the bakery, maybe now instead of a bakery we can have a mud taco restaurant.

Child 2: Yeah, and we can have an oven to cook the tacos.

Child 3: And I can make the menu.

Child 4: But I can be the money person when people want to come and eat in the restaurant. Well, you know, we have to build a table and chairs.

Child 5: That will be easy. I know how to build it.

Child 6: And I want to put a tablecloth on the table with the candles we use when we eat lunch every day in school, and don't worry, Miss Christina. We don't even need your help.

Child 7: But you can watch us and take notes like you always do.

Child 8: And you can take pictures with your camera, too.

Elizabeth Cottino and Cindy Gennarelli, William Paterson University
Child Development Center, Wayne, New Jersey

Describe, Interpret, and Expand on What Children Do and Say

Just being present while children play with blocks and responding appreciatively to their efforts will show children that you value their building. Describing what you see (for example, "the garage you built is just big enough for four cars") provides additional confirmation that you are truly paying attention to their work. At times it may not be clear to you what children are saying or building, so it may be necessary to ask them directly or to help them clarify their thinking by reading back their words to them. Some children may not have a wide enough vocabulary to describe or interpret what they are building. Taking this important step will lead to rich opportunities to expand on the ideas children are exploring in the block area.

Ms. Nicole shares an example of expanding on children's learning in the following anecdote.

As we observe the children creating new constructions and using the open-ended materials, I look for ways to expand their play. I often introduce nonfiction books on topics related to children's interests or take them on virtual field trips using the iPad. The iPad allows me to show children videos and pictures. These inspire the children with more ideas and help the children extend their thinking. For example, when Tuaha was creating the ocean using the sea glass, I used a video to show him how a boat maneuvers through the water and show him different types of boats. Then he chose to make his boat that takes people from place to place.

Nicole Dennis, Paterson, New Jersey

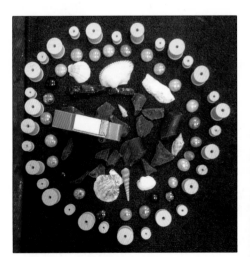

In addition to taking obvious safety measures when using the Internet, you should also be cautious not to always go immediately to the Internet. Encourage children to rely on their own ideas and resources instead of depending on you or the Internet for answers.

Support Language and Vocabulary

When children are engaged in block play, they are highly motivated to communicate and to try out new words. Here preschool teacher Ms. Spadola transcribes children's language during the woodworking project detailed in chapter 5.

During the children's play, I wrote down parts of their conversations, capturing their language "as is" except to offer a prompt for children to describe a shape they held or to ask how they could use the shape. I was mindful not to focus too much on having the children name the shapes and instead listened intently, noticing that their play was highly imaginative.

Aubrey and James build alongside each other for twenty-five minutes.

Aubrey: Miss Spadola, Miss Spadola! A bridge, water under the bridge. This one can be the water. This is curved. I can make a "C" without a marker. I'll choose the curved one.

James: Here is the wheels. I made a car. I got to drive it. I have to add a little bit more. I need a cylinder, a different kind of wheel. This one—I add this one for the bridge. I need something else to hold it. There, that's better. What about my wheels? They fell off my car . . .

As I listened and wrote down children's words, I noticed that they were using a lot of self-talk that included vocabulary that I had not heard them use before. This explosion of words was a surprise to me, but also a confirmation of the value of this *activity in helping children build language and use more sophisticated vocabulary. I also noticed that children made visual analogies when they intentionally selected blocks to represent another item, which Brielle and Rayanna demonstrated so perfectly in the next example. I am more convinced now that using objects in this creative way helps children develop more sophisticated abstract thinking skills than when they use commercial toys or accessories for a closed-ended purpose.*

Brielle and Rayanna work together for forty-five minutes.

Brielle: That's the dad, because he's bigger.

Rayanna: This is the baby birthday cake.

Brielle: This is the mommy birthday cake.

Brielle: I got it to balance.

Rayanna: Look, the daughter and the two babies.

Brielle: We still have to get two drinks. That's the candles. This looks like chocolate. Lipstick . . . Mommy, I found your lipstick.

Rayanna: Look, I found a snowman baby toy.

Brielle: The tea, the ice tea. Everyone is hiding.

Rayanna: Yeah, for the birthday. They can't see her.

Building falls.

Rayanna: Ugh. See, Brielle!

Brielle: Oops, I'll do it again.

Both girls immediately begin to rebuild.

Brielle: Look, Rayanna, another big plate. We found a lot of plates.

Rayanna: The mommy has the yummy stuff. Pie. We need more people.

Both girls search through bin for cylinders with spheres on top.

Rayanna: When one plate is dirty, you can get more from here.

Brielle (singing): Plates and plates and plates.

Rayanna: The mommy wants to lay down. She is tired.

Brielle: Someone passed away. Oh, now we need baby plates.

Rayanna: Let's find more and more and more plates.

The girls add pieces without talking for a few minutes.

Rayanna: I'm tired. Let's build something nicer.

Teacher: Let's look at what you built from all sides before we clean it up.

Brielle: It looks messy on this side and clean on this side.

Kathleen Spadola, Paterson, New Jersey

Point Out Building Elements, Concepts, and New Terms

As we saw in chapter 1, block play offers children the opportunity to learn many important concepts and terms related to social studies, mathematics, science, engineering, architecture, and construction. Providing children with the appropriate term at the moment when they connect it to an action makes the learning more meaningful and something they will not likely forget.

Ms. Calafut feels that the children are ready to investigate the science behind constructing strong buildings. She introduces a more in-depth, long-term study of the effects of a force (wind) on the structures children have built. She reads The Three Little Pigs. *The children work in teams to build structures out of straws and connectors, foam blocks, and wood blocks. They make predictions based on their experiences with building and vote on which structure they think will be the strongest. Then they test each of the structures (with a fan) and find that the wooden blocks are the strongest, just like the brick house in the story of the pigs.*

In the course of the study, children develop a growing awareness of the effects that forces such as wind have on different types of construction and a deeper understanding of what it means to build strong, stable buildings. Ms. Calafut supports this learning by joining the children on the floor during their play to reinforce

the concepts and terms they are learning. In addition, she places drawing paper, pencils, and books on construction in the block area, along with photographs of familiar buildings and bridges in the community. The result is that the children are immersed in the many languages of building: books, photographs, and drawing and building materials.

Ms. Calafut reflects, "Children in my class this year learned that their work as builders is important and valued. They developed many science inquiry skills and builder's behaviors. I learned that there is unlimited opportunity to use block building to teach science and math. I believe we have laid the foundation for the work ahead."

Arlene Calafut, New Brunswick School District, New Brunswick, New Jersey

In these photos, Mrs. Calafut observes that the children in her classroom are highly engaged in building tall towers. In their play, she notices that the children understand that to build stable towers that don't fall over, they have to construct their towers with strong, sturdy foundations. She provides illustrated books, photos and targeted vocabulary to assist these English Language Learners in applying scientific language and concepts, such as stability and balance, as they build.

Make Connections with Other Areas of Learning and Life

Block play helps children make connections to other areas of life. In this vignette, Jayde makes connections with an experience she has had with farm animals. She first plans the materials needed to construct a farm with minimal support from her teacher. She creates a farm step-by-step using unit blocks, found materials, and farm animals. Then she documents her completed structure using the classroom block journal.

Jayde enters the block center and says, "I'm going to make a house. You help make me a farm. We need animals so they can come out. Maybe we can make a building like a animals."

Not understanding Jayde's comment after asking for clarification, Ms. Nicole responds, "Do you mean, can we make a building for the animals?"

Jayde then says, "A house so they can't get lost." She lays the animals down and says, "They going to nap."

Encouraging Reflection

> The very private musing of a child finds its origins in wonder and may eventually be transformed through reflection, dialogue, and finally collaboration into a question and ultimately a theory about the world.
>
> **Karen Gallas, *Talking Their Way into Science: Hearing Children's Questions and Theories, Responding with Curricula***

Reflection is a process for remembering and thinking about your actions. When adults engage children in reflection, it helps children become more aware of their thinking and what they have learned. By drawing, writing, singing, acting out, sharing, or talking about their experiences, children get in touch with how they feel about the process or topic. They discover what interests them and take a more active role in building on or extending their experience. Reflection also helps children connect what they learn to other situations, which leads to more informed decisions and evaluations (Epstein 2003; Nell, Drew, and Bush 2013).

Have Children Draw What They Build

> The act of constructing seems to give children both visual and tactile understanding of form. Once children build a structure, they seem quite comfortable trying to draw it. The experience is a powerful one for children. It is a great way to help children realize and become aware of their potential and ability.
>
> **Cathy Weisman Topal and Lella Gandini, *Beautiful Stuff!***

Drawing helps children become more careful observers. Children learn to look closely at their constructions—specifically at the shapes within the structure—often noticing new details they might not have seen before. Drawing helps children translate three-dimensional construction to two-dimensional paper and vice versa, which architects and builders often do when they create and refer to blueprints.

Block construction allows children to develop and practice many different skills simultaneously, but by drawing the structures, children enhance their visual-spatial skills in particular. It is common for children to communicate what they know through their drawings before they have the ability to verbalize that knowledge. This makes drawing an especially useful tool for children with language delays and those who are English-language learners (Miller 2004).

Melanie re-creates a building she finds in a book, then draws it.

Children in Ms. Spadola's class draw their wood constructions.

Encourage Multiple Ways for Children to Express Their Ideas and Thinking

> When children represent ideas through building, dramatic play, storytelling, drawing, painting, clay work, and three-dimensional sculptures, dance, and music, they show us they understand something about symbolic thinking, a cornerstone of meaningful literacy.
>
> **Deb Curtis and Margie Carter,** *Designs for Living and Learning*

Ms. Nicole attended a workshop at the local university called "Voices of the Land," which helped her realize that children's voices should be nurtured not only in the art center but also in the science and block areas. Although she often encouraged children's language through fingerplays, movement games, and a variety of props and prompts during read-alouds and dramatic play, she felt challenged to encourage children's expressive languages through loose parts and natural materials to create, photograph, and write about their own work.

Ms. Nicole says, "I sat next to Ava as she was exploring the new materials I had introduced. I asked her to tell me about her creation, and she began describing what she was making. I reminded her about the poem we wrote about a tree and asked Ava if she would like to make a poem about her creation. She smiled and responded 'yes.' I documented this poem by Ava."

Summer
Sweaty
No jacket
No sweater
Dress

Fall
Leaves come down
Red or orange
Color
Cool
Sweater

Winter
Freezing
Sweater
Jacket
Scarf
Hat

Spring

A lot of flowers

Pick them

For your house

For your mommies and
daddies

Decorations

Flowers

Table

Collect rose

Hurt you with thorns

They protect themselves
from people

And other creatures

From eating them.

The end

Revisit Displays of Children's Work

When documentation is displayed, it shows children that their efforts are valued and reminds them of what they have learned. It not only encourages children to revisit their thinking, but it also helps them to reconsider and perhaps change their thinking and thus expand their understanding.

Provide Regular Time for Discussion

It is important to make reflection a regular part of the day, preferably right after choice or center time when children have completed their building. Ms. Nicole shares, "One strategy we use to support reflection is group discussions. Group discussions allow the children time to talk about their ideas. We record their ideas on charts and use visual supports to help struggling children recall new vocabulary." Ms. Spadola calls children together to help sort wood shapes. This actively involves children in the process of comparing and categorizing shapes.

Model and Coach Respectful Listening and Sharing

It always amazes me when I walk into a classroom like Ms. Crumrine's, where children have learned to listen to one another respectfully. This doesn't happen all by itself. Ms. Crumrine makes sure that children understand what the expectations are for group sharing, and she creates a culture and climate where children's contributions are truly valued. Here are a few key strategies I have observed and learned from experts over the years for reflecting on practice with children during group sharing (Gallas 1995; Jalongo 2008):

- Limit the amount of time children are expected to listen with the whole group. This amount can vary by time of day and year. An experienced adult will be able to gauge the attention of the group.
- Model for children what it means to show respect for a speaker by looking at the speaker, being quiet when the person is speaking, and asking thoughtful questions.
- Give your full attention when a child is speaking, and limit distractions. This is becoming more difficult in classrooms today, but children know when they are not being heard, and they will act out accordingly.
- Vary your groupings. Pairing children with partners or in groups of three to five allows all children to speak and listen. It is especially helpful for children who may be timid about speaking in front of a whole group to practice their oral skills.
- Record important questions or observations on chart paper. Keep these posted in the classroom to revisit as needed.
- Teach children the difference between a comment and a question. In Ms. Crumrine's room, Karolyn had finished reading a page from her journal about the train station she built and asked if anyone had a question. Plutarco raised his hand to say that he and Kingston built a bridge. Ms. Crumrine reminded Plutarco that what he contributed was a comment and asked him, "Do you have a question for Karolyn about her train station?"
- Coach children on developing respectful talk behaviors. This takes patience, time, and a keen understanding of the personalities in the group. For example, as Jezhaly was sharing her construction with the group, Ms. Crumrine had to remind two boys not to interrupt. She stressed that an important responsibility of group members is to appreciate and acknowledge others' contributions.

- Help children who dominate discussions learn how to take turns. Teach children who have trouble entering discussions signals they can use to let others know they want to speak. Some children will need gentle reminders to stay on point or to project their voices so that they will be heard. When children are proudly sharing their work, they are highly motivated to communicate effectively.

Improvising, Innovating, and Imagining

In pre-packaged curriculums, even the good ones, the needs of all children cannot be met. Children talk about God, love, life, death, war, blood—BIG THINGS—these are not found in traditional curriculums.

Loris Malaguzzi, "How Children Construct Knowledge"

I am not a chef, but I love to eat and appreciate the art of putting together a beautiful meal. In response to reading a recent review of a cookbook by Russell Moore and Allison Hopelain in the *New York Times* (Adler 2015), I realized that creative teaching can be a lot like being an innovative chef. Sure, you can precisely follow a recipe and manage to produce a well-prepared dish, but when you embrace the unexpected, as these chefs do, the results can be spectacular. "Until now," they say in the introduction, "we've had nothing written down, even dishes we make repeatedly," because "on some level, every meal here needs to feel like it's being made for the first time," warding off "a certain rigidity that can creep into the kitchen."

When teachers rely solely on the type of prepackaged curriculum that Loris Malaguzzi, founder of the Reggio Emilia approach, refers to, a certain rigidity can creep into the classroom. Teaching young children requires a great deal of flexibility and a certain degree of willingness to be comfortable with the unexpected. While being organized and prepared is extremely important, early childhood teacher educator Carrie Lobman stresses that to become more responsive to children's ideas, unexpected events, and unplanned learning opportunities, you sometimes have to be able to improvise and let go of your well-made plans (Lobman 2003).

I remember the day when, as a young teacher, I scrapped all my lesson plans following a special school presentation on kites by the Smithsonian Institution. One of the kites was a simple model children could make. I raced back to my classroom, assembled the materials to make the kites, created a sample kite, and was ready when the children arrived. With the presentation still fresh in their minds, the children were highly motivated to make their kites and were excited to go outside to fly them once we made them. This level of creativity and flexibility didn't happen every day, but having the materials available in advance made it possible often.

The experienced teachers featured in this book offer practical tips for improvising in the classroom and being prepared for unexpected opportunities:

- Have basic construction materials and accessories on hand and available to children during scheduled playtimes. Find a balance between offering an interesting selection of materials and overwhelming children with so much that they don't know where to begin.
- Collaborate with other teachers to borrow, swap, and share materials.
- Take advantage of technology for research on a topic and for documenting what children have created in the block area.
- Survey families early in the year to determine special occupations, hobbies, skills, and interests they may want to share. Let families know when you have a particular need for them to collect materials from home. Items from home provide children with familiar connections to their families and cultures.
- Partner with children and families to organize centers based on new topics of study.
- Search the local public library for information books and storybooks to support a topic of study or a special interest of children.
- Keep prop boxes related to a variety of topics in a closet or outside the classroom for easy access when impromptu needs arise.
- Create mobile containers or request outdoor storage units to hold construction materials during outdoor play.

In the twenty-first century, our world is plagued with challenging problems that require creative solutions. This means that adults need to teach creatively and also encourage children to think creatively by giving them open-ended materials such as blocks. These materials will help children practice solving problems that have no single solution.

In the next chapter, you will notice that the teachers have created environments that feature a wide variety of building materials, as well as an assortment of other open-ended materials that activate children's interests and invite them to participate. The teachers have enriched the experiences by offering related field trips, inviting guests, providing informational books on relevant topics, and extending time to work and reflect as a group. Notice that each phase of these explorations leads to a new interest, question, or challenge—and sometimes a surprising new direction. This is exactly what makes teaching so exciting!

Guiding Deeper Engagement in Block Play

> A child's ability to become deeply absorbed in something, and derive intense pleasure from that absorption, is something adults spend the rest of their lives trying to return to.
>
> **Susan Engel, "Joy: A Subject Schools Lack"**

LONG-TERM STUDIES, PROJECTS, AND INVESTIGATIONS

Children reveal their strengths and capabilities best by constructing knowledge together with other children and their teachers in long-term studies, projects, or investigations. This type of learning by doing and making brings all the subject areas (math, science, language arts, social studies, the arts), domains (physical, social-emotional, and cognitive), and twenty-first-century skills together, resulting in the most powerful and effective type of learning.

The teachers featured in this chapter have approached this deeper process of learning in a variety of ways: by encouraging children to use building and construction materials to represent their ideas and understandings, by noticing the heightened interest of the children during a traditional unit of study, by listening to and documenting conversations during play, by posing questions or problems for children to solve, by inviting children to explore with interesting new materials, and sometimes by intentionally planning provocations.

Posing Provocations

What is a provocation? A provocation is a series of intentional actions taken by a teacher to spark questions, interest, ideas, theories, discussion, or debate in an engaging way that stimulates a child's imagination and thinking. Here are some questions the teachers in this chapter considered in their provocation planning:

- What do children already know about block building?
- What do children talk about and wonder as they are building?
- What do I notice as I observe children building?
- What did I notice specifically about children's social-emotional, physical, cognitive, and language development during the construction process?
- What individual children might need support?
- What do I want each child to learn?
- What role will I play in this block investigation?
- What strategies could I employ to extend and deepen the children's block play?

Choosing a Topic of Study

While it is perfectly acceptable to use a unit of study in a required curriculum as a starting point, it is important to carefully consider a few of the following questions:

- Does the study consider the development of the whole child and the integration of multiple subject areas, or is it focused only on literacy or mathematics? If your goal is to support children in making decisions and becoming more deeply involved in their learning, a single concept removed from meaningful context is not as effective as integrating concepts in multiple content areas in a more relevant way.
- Is the study skills-driven and dependent on workbooks, or does it allow for children's own ideas and questions? Consider how you might encourage initiative, decision making, and creative thinking and allow for mistakes as a place to launch new understanding—not as something to be penalized, scored, or graded.

- Is the study outside the children's direct experience? If so, they will have to rely on the teacher for most of the questions, ideas, information, thinking, and planning.
- Are the expectations for children realistic and attainable, or could the children more easily and efficiently acquire the knowledge and skills later on? While there is a big emphasis today on the theory that earlier is better, this theory is not supported by studies of the effects of academic instruction. When children have more choices in their learning that are grounded in developmentally appropriate experiences, their achievement levels are better in the long run (Katz 2015).
- Does the broad topic in the study take into consideration your community and the cultural backgrounds of the children in your classroom? Although books and visual images provide inspiration and information to inform children's construction, children's firsthand experiences that involve all the senses allow them to bring even greater detail to their building. For example, notice how the children from Ms. Crumrine's classroom in this chapter build sophisticated replicas of buildings and bridges they see every day in their urban community.
- Does the unit of study allow sufficient time for deeper learning? It is important to carve out forty-five to sixty minutes in the daily schedule to ensure that children are not just rushing through the activity. In long-term studies, children need the extended time to apply their knowledge and skills beyond rote learning. When they have this time, they are more apt to show solid understanding of a concept or idea.

Of course, not all children in a class will have the same interest in a topic. Many teachers have found that small groups of five to six children offer the best opportunities for in-depth learning. Keep in mind that children not engaged in the small-group study or investigation will continue their play in other centers or small-group work. Given other options, some children still may not be attracted to the block area. Notice how the teachers in the stories on the following pages encourage children who normally wouldn't be involved in block play by offering interesting, open-ended sensory materials and accessories and unexpected invitations to explore.

SHARING STORIES FROM THE CLASSROOM

Investigating an Idea and a Question: The Right to Protection for Nibbles

Boulder Journey School is a private school in Boulder, Colorado, that welcomes more than two hundred children and their families. Students range in age from six weeks to six years. The school's philosophy of education is inspired by the schools for young children in Reggio Emilia, Italy, and by the work and lives of David and Frances Hawkins. One-third of its teachers are mentors, and two-thirds are interns enrolled in the Boulder Journey School Teacher Education Program, a graduate program and teacher certification program in partnership with the University of Colorado Denver and the Colorado Department of Education. Boulder Journey School considers three categories of children's rights: children's right to protection (from war, abuse, and so on), their right to provisions (food, clean water, clothing, shelter, and so on), and their right to participation.

We support long-term classroom investigations that last several days, weeks, months, and even years. Children can research a topic, concept, or question in depth. Projects focus on meaningful, relevant learning experiences through which children and adults build knowledge together.

Ellen Hall, Desirae Kennedy, Alison Maher, and Lisa Stevens, *Exploring Math and Science in Preschool*

This story begins with the three-year-old children's investigation of the right to protection through construction of animal shelters. Using unit blocks, the children built a barn for the animals using a projected image of a real barn.

This investigation led to the purchase of a class pet, a guinea pig named Nibbles. Once Nibbles arrived in the classroom, the children began to build her various homes using unit blocks.

The children wanted to give gifts to Nibbles, but they were unsure of her favorite color. How do you determine the favorite color of a guinea pig? They devised a plan to wrap unit blocks in various colored materials. They built tracks and bridges with the colored blocks and placed Nibbles nearby to observe and document which color she approached.

The children repeated this experiment several times, finally determining that the color Nibbles approached most often was the color she preferred. As you can see, her favorite color is red!

Introducing Familiar Topics:
Transportation, Travel, and World Culture

Krista Crumrine is a kindergarten teacher at the Eugenio Maria de Hostos Center for Early Childhood Education in Union City, New Jersey. The school houses 330 of the district's three-, four-, and five-year-old students. The remainder attend other elementary schools and private providers around the city. Union City has many students living in poverty—91 percent qualify for free or reduced lunch—and a large percentage of students who are English-language learners. Union City has a full-day kindergarten program, and most kindergarten students participate in the district's full-day preschool and pre-K programs prior to kindergarten. In Mrs. Crumrine's classroom, fourteen students are English-language learners, and two students have Individual-ized Education Programs (IEPs). The classroom has a full-time aide as well as a special education teacher two periods per day. Krista has been teaching kindergarten for eight years using the district's theme-based curriculum, which integrates science and social studies into reading and math and centers on project-based learning. She tells the following story in her own words.

People have always built cities because without cities, everybody would have to stand up all the time and just walk around.
Silvia (age four), *Reggio Tutta: A Guide to the City by the Children.*

The children in my kindergarten classroom like to take off with their own ideas in the block center. It is so interesting to watch and listen as they come up with building plans, build their structures, and then change their ideas numerous times. Having time built into the schedule for children to explore their ideas with blocks increases their confidence in their building abilities.

During our transportation unit this year, the children eagerly contributed to our discussions about world travel. Many of them have done some traveling, even at their young age, since they have family living in other countries. We talked a lot about heritage and culture and then discussed buildings and landmarks. The children loved building famous buildings and bridges. They used books and photos to help guide their buildings.

The block center helps me teach science concepts, such as balance, as well as math concepts, such as measurement and geometry. I am fortunate that my blocks have their own space in my classroom, so I have started letting students work on a structure for more than one day so they can really complete it how they want. I also let them keep it built for a day or two. They give other students "tours" of their buildings and explain different parts. This is great for their listening and speaking skills. The rest of the class loves to ask questions. I also posted the photos I took of the students on the wall in the block center as a discussion piece once the structure was taken apart.

For the hundredth day of school, the boys counted out one hundred blocks to see what they could build with them. They built a train station, which is pictured from the front and from the interior. They said, "We made a train station. The high-speed train just came by to pick up the people. They are going to California. They point to the bathroom. We couldn't think of anyplace else to be the bathroom."

"It is a train museum. It is where they take trains when they are old."

Anushka and Jezhaly identified their structure in this photo as a building from New York City with a road around it. Both girls are generally very quiet and shy, but I was able to observe them communicating very well as they built this structure. The use of blocks gave them a great opportunity for teamwork and communication.

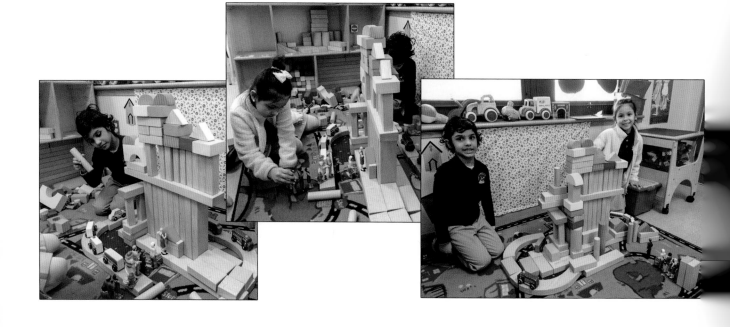

These boys are working together to build a gym and then sketch their building.

During our "Around the World" unit, we discussed the different cultures of the children in our classroom as well as important buildings and landmarks. This connected to literature as well as math (geometry). In the following photo, Karolyn and Remy have built the White House, complete with a fountain in front.

Given our proximity to New York City, our children have had many firsthand experiences with bridges and buildings. In the following two photos, Plutarco and Kingston are building a bridge. It took them many tries to figure out a way to balance their structure. I was able to watch them build and have their bridge fall. Then they discussed how they would get it to stand up, figuring out a way to make it stabler. The boys worked as a team to figure out a plan, learning persistence while also meeting specific standards. In the end, they built a bridge for cars and one for people. They even used the blue foam blocks to show that there was water under the bridge.

The two children in the following photo said, "We made a trampoline (indoors). There was a fire on the top. There are some people outside looking at it. It is closed." Most of the time I hear my students speaking English, but when I listen to them in the block center, I notice that some students switch back and forth between English and their home language depending on their partner.

Taking on New Perspectives: The Bird Blind

The William Paterson University Child Development Center (now closed) was located on the university campus in Wayne, New Jersey. The NAEYC-accredited center had the underpinnings of Reggio Emilia and encouraged children to be the protagonists and researchers in their own learning. Since provocations came from the children's interests, they explored and investigated in meaningful, developmentally appropriate ways. The center was a one-room classroom that accommodated preschool children, ages three years to six years. It was open to children of William Paterson University faculty, staff, students, and alumni. The center was a program of the university's college of education, and it served as a laboratory site for faculty, undergraduate, and graduate student research and course work. It also provided a place for undergraduate students to fulfill their practicum and student teaching experiences. Both the director, Cindy Gennarelli, and the lead teacher, Elizabeth Cottino, taught university undergraduate- and graduate-level early childhood education classes. Other staff members included teachers with master's degrees, graduate assistants, and student workers.

While some may want people who do not ask questions but rather follow commands without thinking, Duckworth emphasizes that many others want people who are confident in what they do, who do not just follow what they are told, who see potential and possibility, and who view things from different perspectives.

Walter F. Drew and Baji Rankin, "Promoting Creativity for Life Using Open-Ended Materials"

One morning in early April, Ms. Liz began circle time with the following question:

Ms. Liz: Boys and girls, I was wondering if you could help me identify this bird I heard in my yard this morning.

Child 1: Okay, Ms. Liz, we can do it. We are bird experts, you know. We are ornithologists right now, and we are doing bird rescue.

Ms. Liz: Well, this was the sound I heard: *tap, tap, tap.*

Child 2: Maybe give us another clue.

Ms. Liz: The sound was coming from a very tall evergreen tree.

Child 1: Well, it couldn't be a chickadee, because it said *tap, tap, tap*, not *chickadee-dee-dee*.

Child 3: And I know it wasn't a robin, because it said *tap, tap, tap*, not *cherrilee*.

Child 4: And I even know it wasn't a blue jay, because it didn't say *jay, jay, jay*.

Child 5: Hey, wait a minute, I know what it was. It has to be a woodpecker because they tap, tap, tap. They don't say *tap, tap, tap*, but they make that noise with their beak. Ms. Liz, was it a drumming sound or a tapping sound?

Ms. Liz: I am not sure, because when I tried to get closer, the bird flew away.

Child 2: Well, why didn't you use a bird blind? You know, you could make one just like the one we made.

Child 3: Or maybe we can make one for you.

Child 4: Next time bring your binoculars and your camera, Ms. Liz. Just like you always tell us. And you know what else? We need to build a real bird blind and look for birds outside, just like we do in the classroom when we pretend.

Ms. Liz: I think that is a great idea, but what should we use to build the blind?

Child 6: How about real blocks? We can take them all outside and just build the blind. We know how to do it.

Going from Intentions to a Cocreated Project: The Rocket Ship Study

The Kean University Child Care and Development Center (KUCCDC) enrolls children from two and a half to five years of age in four classrooms. KUCCDC has been involved in Reggio-inspired curriculum approaches for the past eight years. The children stay with the same teacher and the same group of children for two years; they learn empathy and build strong relationships with their teachers and with the other children. The center also serves as a site for student teachers to carry out their student teaching practicum. Each semester, student teachers develop an interdisciplinary project with the children in their classroom, based on close observation of the children's interests, while meeting the state standards. Dr. Sonja de Groot Kim, faculty member in the early childhood and family studies program at Kean University, works closely with each student in identifying a possible topic of study after a period of closely observing the children. As the faculty liaison to the center, she meets weekly with the director and teachers to talk about the possible topics and directions for study. The teachers document children's interactions and conversations and outline their tentative plans in weekly plans called "Intentions."

The rocket ship study took place in Laura Masterson's classroom, and the student teacher was Julia Reyes. The children who started in Laura's class when they were two and three years old were, a year later, the protagonists of the rocket ship study. The study lasted for seven months. It even continued after the student teacher had finished her semester, because the children were still very involved and interested. The exciting (and sometimes scary) aspect of studies such as this is that no one ever knows at first how a study may evolve. Teachers and children create projects together, navigating the twists and turns of an exciting journey. Laura and Julia tell the following story in their own words.

The question was not how would I enter [the children's play], but, rather, what were the effects of my intervention? When did my words lead the children to think and say more about their problems and possibilities, and when did my words circumvent the issue and silence the actors? When did my answers close the subject?

Vivian G. Paley, "On Listening to What the Children Say"

To begin this study, we observed children's interest in building rocket ships in the block area over a period of several days. A small group had been creating them in different learning centers. Shaan, Seamus, Henry, Krish, and Abby created a rocket ship in the block area, the meeting area, and in home living. Each structure has been different. Some are rectangular and some are a long line of blocks.

We created a web, writing down what children knew and understood about this topic and questions or wonderings they might have. In the rocket ship study, the provocation was not teacher designed. The play was initiated by the children building in different areas of the classroom.

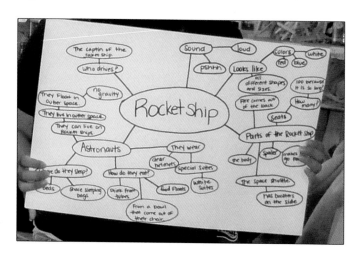

In this classroom, the block center was intentionally set up near the home living area. The children easily flowed back and forth between the two areas and were allowed to bring items to support their investigations. Initially, when the boys used the blocks to create what they called a rocket ship, some girls wanted to join. The boys refused, saying that girls could not be astronauts. The girls withdrew to home living, loudly proclaiming to the boys, "You can't come in here!" Instead of telling the boys to let the girls join, we brought in books about female astronauts to read to the children and left them in the library and the block area. This seemed to empower the girls, because they began to insert themselves into the play by joining the boys and creating a cafeteria where food was prepared and served for the astronauts' "long journey."

The children's excitement about rocket ships blasted off. On Wednesday morning, a small group began working on their rocket. A few more "experts" joined in, saying that the astronauts needed to pack sets of clothes if they were going to be away for a while, and they would need food! Suddenly a cafeteria was being built on as an addition to the rocket ship. The astronauts ate, and more "experts" joined in. Henry made an interesting comment that "astronauts eat through tubes." On Friday, the small group built a new rocket ship where the old one

was, but they removed the rocket ship's cafeteria. Henry's interesting comment about astronauts eating through tubes might have inspired them to do this. We had clear plastic tubes in the rice table and decided to place them near the rocket ship area as a provocation. The children found the tubes and pretended to eat through them. This week we will continue to observe and ask questions.

Both boys and girls spent time in the rocket ship area using clipboards, which had been intentionally left out to encourage children's drawing and beginning writing. We find that when writing implements are left in different areas of the classroom, children will make use of them. Shaan is drawing a map of where he thinks the rocket ship will blast off. The rectangular unit block was specifically chosen by him to represent a GPS to navigate them through space.

Shaan has left his map on the clipboard and will likely return to it. Ying and Victoria are in deep concentration as they are making a list of food items to collect and bring into the rocket ship.

The children in this classroom know each other quite well, since they were together the year before. They have become experienced block builders, both with unit blocks and with hollow blocks, incorporating other materials, including found materials, into their block play. There is a room in the school we call the "studio," which contains a large variety of recyclable and found materials. Small groups of two to three children made regular trips to the studio with a teacher to select materials to add to their rocket ship block play. Children were heard talking about needing

astronaut masks for their faces in order to breathe, so they were invited to the studio to find something that could represent masks. They found clear plastic salad bowls. The children immediately pronounced that these could be the masks for the astronauts' faces. They spent weeks trying all different ways to attach the masks to their heads, with limited success.

In the black and white photograph, you'll notice other provocations the teachers made accessible, such as keyboards, speakers, and cameras.

Children in the center are encouraged to collaborate with each other, so there are always lively conversations and discussions, which include arguments, problem solving, and negotiating as they work with each other. We noticed that children's vocabulary grew immensely as they learned more and more about rocket ships, outer space, and other planets. They created a variety of items to go into the rocket ship. Often they pretended that one thing represented something else. For example, Shaan had a pillow on his lap that he called his iPad. Henry found a pair of sunglasses in the studio that he repurposed into what he called a "double video game that you need to use inside the rocket ship." Shaan also left a space open and told people not to sit there because he was building the engine and that spot was for "the spoiler" Children talked about needing a GPS to go into space because their parents had one in their car.

Documenting a study or project in a busy classroom is not easy. We always carry a small spiral notebook so that we can jot down key words and then later expand on them during the children's naptime. We also videotape and audiotape interactions and conversations and listen to them when we have an opportunity. Oftentimes we upload a video clip onto our laptops and view it later with the children. This is an excellent way to reflect on what has happened, since we will frequently notice details and/or add other ideas or questions to further the investigation together. We find videotaping to be more effective than audiotaping because the children can be seen and heard; on the audio recording it was too difficult to distinguish children's individual voices. Videotaping children's interactions and conversations during block play is a very effective way to assess children's level of understanding. For example, Lily was wondering, "How do astronauts know when it is time to blast off?" Other children talked about counting down and showed her how that worked. Children also wondered how astronauts go to the bathroom and wash their hands in spaceships. We checked out video clips online as well as books about these matters, which we all watched and discussed together.

Frequently throughout the study, we would meet with an individual child or with small groups of children to discuss their ideas. Children need to have a voice in determining the direction of an investigation, and listening to them—really listening to them—can help further the investigation. Krish was talking to Julia about having a GPS to take on the rocket ship's trip so "we know where to go." Many children had experience with a GPS in their family's car and shared their knowledge about how a GPS shows you which road to take and where to make a turn.

At one of our weekly staff Intentions meetings, we discussed Krish's idea and decided to add a mental provocation. In the morning meeting, we said to the children: "You said that the GPS in your car tells you what road to take and where to make a turn. When you take a GPS into space, how do you know where you're going?" This brought about a spirited conversation (critical thinking), and suddenly the children started talking about stars and planets that would point them in the direction they wanted to go. "Not to the sun," said one child. "That's much too hot."

The rocket ship study lasted from September through March. It started with a long period of block building (two months). After documenting that the children wanted to add "blasters," windows, doors, and a ceiling (for all the "buttons") to

their rocket ship, we decided to bring in a large refrigerator box to see how the children would transform it, using the ideas that they had talked about. The children again spent months on their rocket ship, painting it, counting and adding windows and doors, figuring out how many people would fit, bringing in chairs, deciding who would be the pilots and who would be the passengers on any given day, creating a mural of space with planets and stars, and creating a large picture book about space.

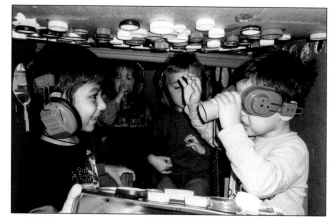

Throughout the seven-month study, all approaches to learning skills were utilized: problem solving, imaginative play, sharing, negotiating, managing frustrations, persistence, invention, concentration, and reflection. Most importantly, children learned that they had ideas, they were listened to respectfully, they engaged in discussions, they tried approaches, and they failed and tried different approaches. They were competent and resilient, capacities that will stand them in good stead in their growing years.

Building on Children's Interests with an Invitation: The Wood Construction Study

This story takes place in a public preschool classroom in Paterson, New Jersey, a district with a high percentage of children living in poverty, many of whom are English-language learners. The teacher of this class of four-year-olds is Kathleen (Katie) Spadola. Katie has taught in both preschool and kindergarten. The children attend preschool for six hours a day and may also attend before- and after-school sessions. There are fifteen children, one of whom has an identified disability, and a full-time aide in Ms. Spadola's classroom. Katie uses a state-required curriculum and child performance assessment, which has helped her become a highly skilled observer of children's learning. This documentation of one classroom project, told in Katie's own words, demonstrates a keen ability to use what she has observed about each child to motivate them to become deeply invested in their own learning.

I have found that this idea of testing possibilities is where the richness of an experience with materials lies. It is the time when children build relationships with materials and try out a multitude of ideas.

Cathy Weisman Topal, "Bringing the Spirit of the Studio into the Classroom"

Like many early childhood teachers, I have learned to balance the diverse needs of the children in my classroom with a curriculum that includes comprehensive state standards for all preschoolers. This documentation of an intellectually engaging exploration with children will illustrate one way to build on children's work with blocks in a way that fosters curiosity and creativity while also meeting the standards.

Following a study of buildings in their community, children in my class were provided with many opportunities to replicate familiar buildings in the block area. What interested them most, though, were the construction workers whom they observed building stairs made out of wood during one of their walks in the neighborhood. I took advantage of this interest and invited one of the children's dads, an employee at a local building supply store, to share his tools and skills with the children.

Seeing the children's growing interest in and knowledge of basic wood construction, I arranged a trip to a building supply store. In the lumber section, children observed firsthand a demonstration of wood being cut by a saw. In addition to hearing the sounds of wood being cut, feeling the texture and unique smell of wood, seeing enormous stacks of wood and the tools that builders needed to work with wood, the children's senses were engaged in a way that would be impossible to experience through a book or even on digital media with sound. For this group of children, it was just the motivation they needed for the next step of this investigation.

Back in the classroom, the children drew impressions and memories of their trip to the store.

In the past, I might have ended the study there, but having scouted out a place to get free wood scraps, I decided to introduce wood scraps to the classroom for the children to explore. I charted children's words as they interacted with the wood scraps and shared photographs and books about where wood comes from and how loggers bring the trees to lumber mills, where they are transformed into building materials. Here is a list of those words:

3-D	cube	level	sculpture
angle	curved	lumber	sphere
architect	design	organize	symmetrical
arrange	edge	permanent	symmetry
base	gallery	planking	temporary
cone	hammer	rough	timber
construct	knot	sawdust	view

Thinking about next steps for this investigation that would honor the children's interests, I decided against a study of different types of wood and the trees they came from, and focused on the properties of wood. I introduced different grades of sandpaper, which was a new way to learn about sequencing, and I gave children time to sand the rough wood scraps. Allowing children time to look for knots with magnifying glasses, examine the features of each shape, compare finished wood to a recently cut tree, and notice the saw-dust created from sanding deepened their understanding of the special properties of wood.

Once the wood was sanded to a smooth touch, the children had the idea of painting the wood. This posed new challenges in moving and manipulating the larger scraps, giving them opportunities to problem solve and work cooperatively together.

Books used in Katie's wood construction project:

Architecture Shapes by Michael J. Crosbie

Beautiful Oops! by Barney Saltzberg

Block City by Robert Louis Stevenson

Bruno the Carpenter by Lars Klinting

Changes, Changes by Pat Hutchins

Cubes, Cones, Cylinders, and Spheres by Tana Hoban

The Giving Tree by Shel Silverstein

Houses and Homes by Ann Morris

Old MacDonald Had a Workshop by Lisa Shulman

Roberto: The Insect Architect by Nina Laden

Shapes in Buildings by Rebecca Rissman

Shapes, Shapes, Shapes by Tana Hoban

The Toolbox by Anne Rockwell

Tool Book by Gail Gibbons

When I Build with Blocks by Niki Alling

One day, after dumping the wood scraps on the carpet, the children asked me if they could sort the wood scraps together. Though not planned, the whole group of children became very engaged, taking turns in sorting the wood shapes on large easel paper I set out.

Once the scraps were sorted, the children put the scraps in bins in the newly created woodworking area. I carefully organized this area so the children could easily use the center independently. Because the children participated in organizing the center with me, they really took ownership in how they used it. They made signs for the basket of books about trees and wood we had gathered, and they displayed one of the creations they had made out of wood and recycled materials.

With the center organized and ready, I offered an invitation: "Which pieces of wood interest you?" With this provocation, the children were now free to play with the wood scraps in an open-ended way.

Children worked independently at the woodworking center, with few needing my support—though when they did, I became more selective about how I scaffolded their learning. I was intentional in allowing children this time to explore deeply without interrupting or taking over their play.

It was time to introduce a new challenge to the children. I taught the children a technique for gluing the wood scraps together to make a sculpture based on a rhyme created by Triada Samaras:

Tap, tap, tap
Wipe, wipe, wipe,
Spread, spread, spread,
Like jelly on bread.
(Bisgaier, Samaras, and Russo 2005, 14)

As the gluing began, I noticed a distinct shift. The children were less focused on imaginative play and conversation and were now concentrating on the process of gluing. I think that if I had made glue available too early in the exploration, these important experiences would have been lost. Gluing presented entirely new problem-solving opportunities, such as when Abraham tried to create a see-through window with his scraps.

Respecting the pace of each child while also being aware of school schedule limitations, I allowed the children to work on gluing pieces to their sculpture over several days and allowed them to bring their unfinished sculptures to circle time for discussion. These group sessions became an incredibly valuable time to reflect on and talk about their challenges and to share solutions.

Once the children were satisfied that their constructions were complete, I invited children to revisit their found materials collection, which sparked children's interest in a new direction. Earlier, they had sorted materials by subject, and now chose their favorite objects in another way. For example, favorite ribbons and buttons would now be sorted by color. When this was accomplished, I suggested that the children choose just one color of objects to add to their sculpture. This activity generated another great opportunity for informal conversations using descriptive language.

After putting the finishing touches on their wood constructions, children were asked to do observational drawings using fine-line markers.

The children could then add color to their drawings.

The culmination of the children's explorations with three-dimensional wood construction featured an exhibit of the children's finished work. They created signs and invitations, helped set up the gallery, and responded to questions I had posed:

Question 1: What were you thinking as you built your sculpture? What do you want people to know about your sculpture?

Question 2: What was the most difficult part about creating your wood sculpture? What did you do about it?

The children invited families, staff, and children from other classes to visit the gallery. The visitors were invited to leave notes commenting on sculptures.

This exploration with wood opened many possibilities for learning. Children engaged in complex problem solving, were deeply focused in their work, and learned to become more reflective in the process of creating. They worked cooperatively and respectfully with one another, engaging in informal conversations and self-talk rich in language, and practiced setting boundaries and being more flexible.

Children at every developmental level felt successful. Working in three dimensions opened new windows of understanding that had not been revealed through two-dimensional work alone. Children took great pride in their work and great joy in sharing what they had created with other classes and parents.

Big adventures can grow from very simple beginnings.
Cathy Weisman Topal, "Bringing the Spirit of the Studio into the Classroom"

References

Adler, Tamar. 2015. "The Taste of Serendipity." *New York Times Magazine,* www
.newyorktimes.com/2015/11/15/magazine/the-taste-of-serendipity.html.

Almon, Joan. 2013. "It's Playtime!" *Principal,* September/October: 12–15.

Bisgaier, Corinna S., Triada Samaras, and Michele J. Russo. 2005. "Young Children Try, Try Again Using Wood, Glue, and Words to Enhance Learning." In *Spotlight on Young Children and the Creative Arts,* edited by Derry Koralek, 12–18. Washington, DC: NAEYC.

Bodrova, Elena, and Deborah J. Leong. 2005. "Self-Regulation: A Foundation for Early Learning." *Principal,* September/October: 30–36.

Carter, Margie, and Kristie Norwood. 2016. "Our Work Is More Than Our Job." *Exchange* 38 (3): 8–13.

Chalufour, Ingrid, and Karen Worth. 2004. *Building Structures with Young Children.* Saint Paul, MN: Redleaf Press.

Conn-Powers, Michael. 2006. "All Children Ready for School: Approaches to Learning." *Early Childhood Briefing Paper Series.* Bloomington: Indiana University Press.

Copple, Carol, and Sue Bredekamp, eds. 2009. *Developmentally Appropriate Practice in Early Childhood Programs: Serving Children from Birth through Age 8.* Washington, DC: NAEYC.

Curtis, Deb, and Margie Carter. 2015. *Designs for Living and Learning: Transforming Early Childhood Environments.* Limited ed. Saint Paul, MN: Redleaf Press.

Daly, Lisa, and Miriam Beloglovsky. 2015. *Loose Parts: Inspiring Play in Young Children.* Saint Paul, MN: Redleaf Press.

Dauksas, Linda, and Jeanne White. 2014. "Discovering Shapes and Space in Preschool." *Teaching Young Children* 7 (4): 22–26.

Dewar, Gwen. 2011–12. "Improving Spatial Skills in Children and Teens: Evidence-Based Activities and Tips." *Parenting Science.* www
.parentingscience.com/spatial-skills.html.

Dombro, Amy Laura, Judy Jablon, and Charlotte Stetson. 2011. *Powerful Interactions: How to Connect with Children to Extend Their Learning.* Washington, DC: NAEYC.

Drew, Walter F., and Baji Rankin. 2005. "Promoting Creativity for Life Using Open-Ended Materials." In *Spotlight on Young Children and the Creative Arts,* edited by Derry Koralek, 32–39. Washington, DC: NAEYC.

Edwards, Carolyn, Lella Gandini, and George Forman, eds. 1993. *The Hundred Languages of Children: The Reggio Emilia Approach to Early Childhood Education.* Norwood, NJ: Ablex Publishing.

Elkind, David. 2009. "Introduction to the 25th Anniversary Edition" in *The Hurried Child.* Cambridge, MA: DaCapo Press.

Engel, Susan. 2015. "Joy: A Subject Schools Lack." *The Atlantic.* www.theatlantic.com/education/archive/2015/01/joy-the-subject-schools-lack/384800/.

Epstein, Ann S. 2003. "How Planning and Reflection Develop Young Children's Thinking Skills." *Beyond the Journal: Young Children on the Web*, September. www.naeyc.org/files/yc/file/200309/Planning&Reflection.pdf.

Gallas, Karen. 1995. *Talking Their Way into Science: Hearing Children's Questions and Responding with Theories with Curricula.* New York: Teachers College Press.

Gardner, Howard. 1983. *Frames of Mind: The Theory of Multiple Intelligences.* New York: Basic Books.

———. 2010. "The Nurturance of Artistic Creativity: Lessons from the Study of Creative Exemplars." Keynote at the Educating the Creative Mind Conference, Kean University, Union, NJ, March 3–5.

Giles, Rebecca M., and Karyn W. Tunks. 2015. "A Block Journal: Building Young Authors through Construction Play." *Exchange* 221 (32): 32–35.

Golbeck, Susan L. 2005. "Building Foundations for Spatial Literacy in Early Childhood." *Young Children* 60 (6): 72–83.

Goldsworthy, Andy. 1990. *A Collaboration with Nature.* New York: Harry N. Abrams.

Gramling, Michael. 2015. *The Great Disconnect in Early Childhood Education.* Saint Paul, MN: Redleaf Press.

Grossman, Sue. 1996. "The Worksheet Dilemma: Benefits of Play-Based Curricula." *Early Childhood News.* www.earlychildhoodnews.com/earlychildhood/article_view.aspx?ArticleId=134.

Gullo, Dominic F., ed. 2006. *K Today: Teaching and Learning in the Kindergarten Year.* Washington, DC: NAEYC.

Hall, Ellen, Desirae Kennedy, Alison Maher, and Lisa Stevens. 2015. "Exploring Trees" in *Exploring Math and Science in Preschool.* Washington, DC: NAEYC.

Hanscom, Angela J. and Richard Louv. 2016. *Balanced and Barefoot: How Unrestricted Outdoor Play Makes for Strong, Confident, and Capable Children.* Oakland: New Harbinger Publications.

Harms, Thelma, Richard M. Clifford, and Debby Cryer. 2015. *Early Childhood Environment Rating Scale.* 3rd ed. New York: Teachers College Press.

Hirsch, Elisabeth S., ed. 1996. *The Block Book.* 3rd ed. Washington, DC: NAEYC.

Hyson, Marilou. 2008. *Enthusiastic and Engaged Learners: Approaches to Learning in the Early Childhood Classroom.* New York: Teachers College Press.

Jalongo, Mary Renck. 2008. *Learning to Listen, Listening to Learn.* Washington, DC: NAEYC.

Katz, Lilian G. 2015. "Lively Minds: Distinctions between Academic versus Intellectual Goals for Young Children." *Defending the Early Years.* https://deyproject.files.wordpress.com/2015/04/dey-lively-minds-4-8-15.pdf.

Lobman, Carrie. 2003. "The Bugs Are Coming! Improvisation and Early Childhood Teaching." *Young Children* 58 (3): 18–23.

Lowenfeld, Viktor, and W. Lambert Brittain. 1970. *Creative and Mental Growth.* 5th ed. New York: Macmillan.

Lubinski, David. 2013. "Early Spatial Reasoning Predicts Later Creativity and Innovation, Especially in STEM Fields." *Science Daily,* July 15.

Malaguzzi, Loris. 1993a. "History, Ideas, and Basic Philosophy: An Interview with Lella Gandini." In *The Hundred Languages of Children,* edited by Carolyn Edwards, Lella Gandini, and George Forman, 41–89. Norwood, NJ: Ablex Publishing.

———. 1993b. "How Children Construct Knowledge." Author's notes, lecture, Reggio Emilia Symposium, Washington, DC, June.

———. 1993c. "Hypothesis about the Creative Potential." Author's notes, lecture, Reggio Emilia Symposium, Washington, DC, June.

Miller, Dana L. 2004. "More Than Play: Children Learn Important Skills through Visual-Spatial Work!" Dimensions Educational Research Foundation. www.dimensionsfoundation.org/assets/morethanplayarticle.pdf.

Nell, Marcia L., Walter F. Drew, and Deborah E. Bush. 2013. *From Play to Practice: Connecting Teachers' Play to Children's Learning.* Washington, DC: NAEYC.

Nemeth, Karen. 2012. *Basics of Supporting Dual Language Learners: An Introduction for Educators of Children from Birth through Age 8.* Washington, DC: NAEYC.

Newburger, Abigail, and Elizabeth Vaughan. 2006. *Teaching Numeracy, Language, and Literacy with Blocks.* Saint Paul, MN: Redleaf Press.

Newcombe, Nora. 2010. "Picture This: Increasing Math and Science Learning by Improving Spatial Thinking." *American Educator,* Summer 2010, 29–43.

Ohio Voices for Learning. 2009. "Where Ideas Learn to Fly." Ohio Voices for Learning. http://ohiovoices.org.

Paley, Vivian G. 1986. "On Listening to What the Children Say." *Harvard Educational Review* 56 (2): 122–31.

Pink, Daniel. 2005. *A Whole New Mind: Moving from the Information Age to the Conceptual Age.* New York: Riverhead Books.

Pollman, Mary Jo. 2010. *Blocks and Beyond: Strengthening Early Math and Science Skills through Spatial Learning.* Baltimore, MD: Brookes.

Project Zero and Reggio Children. 2001. *Making Learning Visible: Children as Individual and Group Learners.* Reggio Emilia, Italy: Reggio Children.

Quenqua, Douglas. 2013. "Study Finds Spatial Skill Is Early Sign of Creativity." *New York Times,* July 15.

Reggio Children. 2000. *Reggio Tutta: A Guide to the City by the Children.* Reggio Emilia, Italy: Reggio Children.

Robinson, Ken, and Lou Aronica. 2015. *Creative Schools: The Grassroots Revolution That's Transforming Education.* New York: Viking.

Society for Research in Child Development. 2013. "Teacher-Child Interactions Support Kids' Development in Different Areas." *ScienceDaily.* www .sciencedaily.com/releases/2013/11/131121091506.htm.

Sorby, Sheryl A. 1999. "Developing 3-D Spatial Visualization Skills." *Engineering Design Graphics Journal* 63 (2): 21–32.

Strauss, Valerie, and Angela Hanscom. 2014. "Why So Many Kids Can't Sit Still in School Today." *Washington Post.* www.washingtonpost.com/news/ answer-sheet/wp/2014/07/08/why-so-many-kids-cant-sit-still-in-school-today/.

Teachstone/CLASS. 2014. "Teacher-Child Interactions in Early Childhood: Research Summary." Teachstone Training. http://cdn2.hubspot.net/hub /336169/file-1265335269-pdf/PDF.

Tomlinson, Heather Biggar, and Hyson, Marilou. 2012. "Cognitive Development in the Preschool Years." In *Growing Minds: Building Strong Cognitive Foundations in Early Childhood.* Washington, DC: NAEYC.

Tompkins, Mark. 1991. "Spatial Learning: Beyond Circles, Squares, and Triangles." In *Supporting Young Learners*, vol. 1, by Nancy Brickman and Lynn Taylor, 215–22. Ypsilanti, MI: High/Scope Press.

Topal, Cathy Weisman. 2005. "Bringing the Spirit of the Studio into the Classroom." In *In the Spirit of the Studio: Learning from the Atelier of Reggio Emilia.* New York: Teachers College Press.

Topal, Cathy Weisman, and Lella Gandini. 1999. *Beautiful Stuff! Learning with Found Materials.* Worcester, MA: Davis.

Tunks, Karyn W. 2009. "Block Play: Practical Suggestions for Common Dilemmas." *Dimensions of Early Childhood.* 37 (1): 3–8.

———. 2013. "Happy 100th Birthday, Unit Blocks!" *Young Children* 68 (5): 82–87.

Uttal, David, Nathaniel G. Meadow, Elizabeth Tipton, Linda L. Hand, Alison R. Alden, Christopher Warren, and Nora S. Newcombe. 2013. "The Malleability of Spatial Skills: A Meta-Analysis of Training Studies." *Psychological Bulletin* 139 (2): 352–402.

Wellhousen, Karyn, and Judith Kieff. 2001. *A Constructivist Approach to Block Play in Early Childhood.* Albany, NY: Delmar.

Additional Resources

Aghayan, Carol, Cate Heroman, and Kai-lee Berke. 2010. *The Creative Curriculum for Preschool Teaching Guide: Featuring the Buildings Study.* Washington, DC: Teaching Strategies.

Bohart, Holly, Kathy Charner, and Derry Koralek, eds. 2015. *Spotlight on Young Children: Exploring Play.* Washington, DC: NAEYC.

Cadwell, Louise Boyd. 2003. *The Reggio Approach: Bringing Learning to Life.* New York: Teachers College Press.

Christenson, Lee Ann, and Jenny James. 2015. "Building Bridges to Understanding in a Preschool Classroom: A Morning in the Block Center." *Young Children* 70 (1): 26–31.

Colker, Laura J. 2014. "Supporting One and All in the Block Center." *Teaching Young Children* 7 (4): 16–17.

Copeland, Sherry, M. Galin, and Sydney Schwartz. 2007. "Strengthening the Teaching Role during Center Time: A Model for Growth." Presentation at the annual conference of the National Association for the Education of Young Children, Chicago, November.

Duckworth, Eleanor. 1996. *The Having of Wonderful Ideas and Other Essays on Teaching and Learning.* 2nd ed. New York: Teachers College Press.

Durham, Sean. 2015. "Blocks: 'Standard' Equipment for Today's Primary Classrooms." *Young Children* 70 (1): 52–58.

Field, Sherry L., and Michelle Bauml. 2014. "Lucy Sprague Mitchell: Champion for Experiential Learning." *Young Children* 69 (4): 94–97.

Ferguson, Marilyn. 1980. "Flying and Seeing: New Ways to Learn." In *The Aquarian Conspiracy: Personal and Social Transformation in Our Time,* 279–321. Los Angeles: J. P. Tarcher.

Gandini, Lella, Lynn Hill, Louise Cadwell, and Charles Schwall, eds. 2005. *In the Spirit of the Studio: Learning from the Atelier of Reggio Emilia.* New York: Teachers College Press.

Ham, Sandra, William A. Firestone, and Rosanne Regan Hansel. 2006. "Early Childhood Education Professional Development Component Study." MSPnet. http://hub.mspnet.org/index.cfm/13068.

Hansel, Rosanne Regan. 2005. Book Review for *A Whole New Mind*, by Daniel Pink. National Art Education Association, *NAEA News*, 47 (6): 5.

———. 2015. "Bringing Blocks Back to the Kindergarten Classroom." *Young Children* 70 (1): 44–51.

Hendrick, Joanne, ed. 1997. *First Steps toward Teaching the Reggio Way*. Upper Saddle River, NJ: Merrill.

Kolbe, Ursula. 2001. *Rapunzel's Supermarket: All about Young Children and Their Art*. Paddington, Australia: Peppinot Press.

Lee, Joohi, Denise A. Collins, and Linda Winkelman. 2015. "Connecting 2-D and 3-D: Drafting Blueprints, Building, and Playing with Blocks." *Young Children* 70 (1): 32–36.

Lehrer, Jonah. 2012. *Imagine: How Creativity Works*. New York: Houghton Mifflin Harcourt.

Lindeman, Karen Wise, and Elizabeth McKendry Anderson. 2015. "Using Blocks to Develop 21st Century Skills." *Young Children* 70 (1): 36–43.

McGrath, P. H. 2005. "Traditional Materials, Unconventional Experiences." In *In the Spirit of the Studio: Learning from the Atelier of Reggio Emilia*. New York: Teachers College Press.

Miller, Edward, and Joan Almon. 2009. "Crisis in the Kindergarten: Why Children Need to Play in School." College Park, MD: Alliance for Childhood.

New Jersey State Department of Education. 2013. "Preschool Teaching and Learning Standards." State of New Jersey Department of Education. www.state.nj.us/education/ece/guide/standards.pdf.

Pelo, Ann. 2007. *The Language of Art: Inquiry-Based Studio Practices in Early Childhood Settings*. Saint Paul, MN: Redleaf Press.

Strasser, Janis, and Lisa Mufson Koeppel. 2010. "Block Building and Make-Believe for Every Child." *Teaching Young Children* 3 (3): 14–15.

Tepylo, Diane Hobenshield, Joan Moss, and Carol Stephenson. 2015. "A Developmental Look at a Rigorous Block Play Program." *Young Children* 70 (1): 18–25.

Tokarz, Barb. 2008. "Block Play: It's Not Just for Boys Anymore." *Exchange,* May/June: 68–71.

Topal, Cathy Weisman. 2003. *Thinking with a Line*. Worcester, MA: Davis Publications.

White, Jan, and Menna Godfrey. 2015. "Making a Mud Kitchen for Mud Day." *Exchange*, May/June: 74–77.

Wurm, Julianne P. 2005. *Working in the Reggio Way: A Beginner's Guide for American Teachers*. Saint Paul, MN: Redleaf Press; Washington, DC: NAEYC.

Index

Photography Credits

Photograph on page 73 copyright oscity / Thinkstock

Photograph on page 21 (bottom) courtesy of Christy Breiby

Photograph on page 37 (bottom) courtesy of Nancy Brown

Photographs on pages 34 (top), 50 (bottom), 64, 76 (top), and 77 courtesy of Marianne Cane and Samantha Flores

Photographs on pages 7, 12, 53 (top right), 69 (top), 70, 78, 79, 80, 81, 82, 85, and 86 courtesy of Tamara Clark

Photographs on page 65 (top) courtesy of Alex Cruickshank

Photographs on pages 89, 120, 121, 122, 123, and 124 courtesy of Krista Crumrine

Photographs on pages 5, 11. 16, 24, 25, 31, 32, 36, 41 (top left and bottom), 49, 50 (right), 53, 54, 55, 58 (right), 59 (top), 60, 61, 62, 66 (bottom), 87 (top), 88, 92, 94, 98, 103, 105, 106, and 107 courtesy of Nicole Dennis

Photograph on page 37 courtesy of Walter Drew

Photographs on pages 118 and 119 courtesy of Lauren Frazier

Photographs on pages 10, 23 (bottom), 34 (bottom), 50, 51 (bottom right), 52, 68, 96, 97, 126, and 127 courtesy of Cindy Gennarelli

Photographs on pages 101 and 102 courtesy of Sally Kacar

Photograph on page 35 courtesy of Kayla Kolodziyezyk

Photographs on pages 41 (top), 42 (bottom), 70, 76 (bottom), 77 (bottom), and 82 (right) courtesy of Christy Lechner

Photographs on pages 129, 130, 131, 132, and 133 courtesy of Laura Masterson

Photograph on page 18 courtesy of Kelli Pringle

Photograph on page 72 courtesy of Brittney Richter

Photograph on page 67 courtesy of Jennifer Selbitschka

Photographs on pages 8, 9, 15, 23 (right), 33, 40, 43, 51, 57, 58 (left), 65 (bottom), 66 (top), 71, 74, 86 (right), 87 (bottom), 99, 100, 109, 135, 136, 137, 138, 139, 140, 141, and 142 courtesy of Kathleen Spadola

Photograph on page 35 courtesy of Tamara Volckmann

The remaining photographs courtesy of the author